PL DIM

A Love for *Life*

Congressman Henry Hyde and the author of this volume in the East Room of the White House at the signing of the Unborn Victims of Violence Act, April 1, 2004.

A Love for *Life*

Christianity's Consistent Protection of the Unborn

Dennis R. Di Mauro

WIPF & STOCK · Eugene, Oregon

A LOVE FOR LIFE
Christianity's Consistent Protection of the Unborn

Wipf & Stock
A Division of Wipf and Stock Publishers
199 W. 8th Ave., Suite 3
Eugene, OR 97401

www.wipfandstock.com

ISBN 13: 978-1-55635-828-9

Manufactured in the U.S.A.

To the late Dr. Harold O. J. Brown

My professor and advisor at Reformed Theological Seminary,
Co-founder of Care Net, *and champion of the unborn.*

Contents

Acknowledgements

A SPECIAL THANKS TO the *National Pro-Life Religious Council* for providing me the opportunity to tell the story of Christianity's continual pro-life witness. I would also like to thank Ms. Marie Bowen, Ms. Georgette Forney, Rev. Terry Gensemer, Dr. Michael Gorman, Mr. Ernie Ohlhoff, Rev. Randy Sly, Mr. Jay Sonstroem, Rev. Paul Stallsworth, Rev. Ben Sheldon, and Rev. Kirk van der Swaagh, for their input into this project. I am also indebted to my copyeditor Ms. Jeanne Osborne, whose grammatical expertise and style advice has proven invaluable. And as always, I would like to thank my wife Coco, and my daughters Zoey, Lucy, and Veronica for their patience with me throughout the writing of this book. It was their sacrifices which allowed me to serve Christ in both my family and in my work.

Introduction

THE LAST DECADE HAS experienced a resurgence of interest in the abortion question. The passage of the Partial-Birth Abortion Ban Act (including its successful review by the Supreme Court in *Gonzalez v. Carhart*) and the public discussions of the gruesome nature of this type of abortion have raised society's consciousness on the issue and have renewed a national discussion on the sanctity of human life.

The high incidence of abortion in the United States, with an estimated 1.2 million being procured every year, has also raised concerns as to the wisdom of our current national policy of abortion-on-demand. Even many social moderates have begun to question whether the legalization of abortion, which was touted in the 1970s as a humane way to handle crisis pregnancies which were due to rape, incest, or fetal abnormalities, has become instead a vastly overused means of dealing with any unwanted pregnancy.

The political climate has also demonstrated that a large percentage of the U.S. population believes that abortion is morally wrong. The outcome of the 2004 Presidential election was widely reported to be the result of George Bush's ability to carry the "values voter," due to his commitment to ending our nation's current public policy of unfettered abortion. The abortion question also loomed large in the 2008 Republican presidential primaries, with many questioning whether Rudy Giuliani, as a pro-choice candidate, would be able to secure that party's nomination.

This heightened awareness of the abortion debate is now forcing most politicians to take either a pro-choice or pro-life stand. In fact, probably no other issue has so polarized our two largest political parties than the issue of abortion, with the Republicans taking a predominantly pro-life position and Democrats taking a mostly pro-choice position.

It also seems that the reason that abortion has become one of the most prominent social issues of our time, and a highly emotional controversy as well, is because it touches on some of the most important questions in the human experience: What is human life? Is there a God? Can I really be totally free? Don't I have a right, and even the obligation, to live my life according to my personal wishes?

The natural response to such transcendent and ethical questions is to seek the answers from God, or from those who interpret God's revelation here on earth: organized religious groups. Since the vast majority of Americans are Christian, this responsibility falls into the lap of the nation's Christian denominations.

To the average American it seems that Christianity, as a whole, has not arrived at a definitive position on abortion (a perception which will be challenged later in this book). When our average citizen opens her morning newspaper, she sees the debate displayed before her: pro-choicers on the left and pro-lifers on the right. However, the news article provides little guidance about whether abortion is morally right or wrong. And, as she reads further about the subject, it seems that the Christian church, often an ethical guide in many of her decisions, is of no use to her. Sadly, she is told, the church is just as divided as the rest of society on the topic. So our average American is left to fend for herself. She must somehow decide the right answer with little guidance from Christianity, or even from God Himself.

But is our average American really without guidance? Has she gotten all the information she needs on abortion, or has she only received the five second sound bite which leaves her as confused as she was before she heard about the abortion debate? And has God been silent on the abortion question? Has the church really shown a diversity of opinion on the sanctity of life?

Part of the confusion on this subject is that our society has, in the past few centuries, excluded Christian history and doctrine from topics of public discourse. The reasoning for this exclusion has been that, since our population now includes adherents of numerous religions, or even more commonly, no religion at all, sectarian theological analysis is of little use in arriving at a consensus on a disputed topic. Consequently, debates of national and international importance are discussed from a solely secular perspective. With regard to the abortion question, these secular questions include, "When does Life begin?" "Am I too young to start a family?" "If

I didn't intend to become pregnant is it still a child?" and "If I give up my freedom to choose an abortion, will I also lose other rights, such as the right to earn the same wage as a man?"

Sadly, these questions avoid the spiritual dimension which is so vital in determining an answer to any confusing moral question. Because religious tradition is considered to be of little use when arbitrating between two opposing opinions, society often ignores the doctrines of the Christian church, whose counsel has heavily influenced the morality of Western society over the last two thousand years.

This type of reliance on secular decision-making even affects practicing Christians. Christians commonly "buy in" to this type of thinking and abandon clear Christian teaching in making moral decisions. But for believers, a study of the Holy Scripture and a thorough review of the history of the church should be able to determine God's will on the abortion question. The Christian seeks to know, and has every reason to believe, that God has revealed instructions that will guide her to make godly decisions in her life.

My prayer is that this book will provide Christians with the biblical and historical information that they need to make an informed decision on the abortion question. The good news is that God *has* clearly revealed Himself on abortion, as He has on many other contemporary moral issues. Christians can take a great deal of solace in the knowledge that they are not alone in having to make such life and death decisions. Instead, they can be confident that God *will* guide them through the maze of secular debates.

This book will demonstrate that Christianity has been, is now, and will be in the future, a pro-life religion. Chapter 1 will review the pro-life attitudes of the Israelite nation before the time of Christ. This review of the pro-life views of our Jewish forebears will provide a strong foundation for the attitudes on abortion held by the early Christian church. Chapter 2 will look at the strident pro-life witness found in Sacred Scripture, and how Christians can find a pervasive pro-life teaching in the Bible, even though the word "abortion" is never found there. Chapter 3 will present excerpts of the writings of the early Church Fathers, such as Augustine, Jerome, and Basil, to see how they interpreted the Bible in regard to the abortion question. Chapter 4 will review the nearly one thousand year history of the Middle Ages, to explore the institutionalization of the pro-life position through the creation of penance guidelines and canon laws that dealt with the sin of abortion. Chapter 5 will research the abortion views of the Protestant Reformers, such as Luther and Calvin, as well as their counterparts in the Catholic Church during the sixteenth century. Since pro-choice Christian voices today are seen mostly in mainline Protestantism, one would expect that many of the sixteenth-century Protestant reformers would have been pro-choice. This chapter will explore whether this was the case, and will also determine if any of the reformers felt that it was acceptable to end a pregnancy through abortion.

Chapter 6 will feature the writings of today's prominent pro-choice Christians. By this point in the book, we will be able to determine whether their views are consistent with those of the biblical writers and Church Fathers, or whether they have taken a new and unorthodox tack. Chapter 7 will look at the major Christian denominations and provide a history of these denominations' position statements and activism on the abortion question since the 1960s. Chapter 8 will take a hard look at whether a sizable pro-choice voice really exists within the church, and at how pervasive the pro-choice opinion is within Christianity.

The book contains two appendixes as well, which will provide additional data for the reader's use. Appendix I provides recent statements from many American Christian denominations on the abortion question. Appendix II lists the members of the *National Pro-Life Religious Council (NPRC)*, a group devoted to refuting the *Religious Coalition on Reproductive Choice (RCRC)* and other pro-choice Christians groups, in order to prove that Christianity has been solidly pro-life in its past, is pro-life in its present, and will be pro-life in its future.

In short, *A Love for Life* will look at the Bible and entire history of the church to determine if abortion really fulfills the will of God, as many pro-choice Christians believe, or whether abortion is a clearly sinful act. In other words, the goal of this book is to discover the *real* message of the church on abortion. It will begin with a review of the moral attitudes of the Jewish people before the time of Christ. These views heavily influenced sanctity of life ethics within first-century Christianity.

Ancient Traditions

Historical Jewish Views on Abortion

CHRISTIAN DOCTRINE ON THE morality of abortion was to a large degree "inherited" from our Jewish ancestors. Therefore, a review of early Jewish attitudes towards life in the womb is needed to understand later Christian ethical positions on this practice.

Any discussion of Jewish views on abortion often begins with a review of Exodus 21:22–25. This passage provided direction on how to punish a man who had, in the course of a fight with another man, accidentally injured a woman and caused her to have a miscarriage. Much has been made of this passage in the abortion debate, because it is arguably the only verse in the Old Testament which deals with the punishment given to a person who kills an unborn child.

The use of this verse has been complicated by the fact that it has been rendered differently in the ancient Hebrew and Greek texts. In the original Hebrew text, the passage required the violator to pay a fine to the woman's husband in reparation for the unborn child's death. If the assault resulted in the woman's death or injury as well, the text called for an "eye for [an] eye," meaning an equivalent punishment for the perpetrator: his execution if the mother was killed, or a physical punishment if the mother was injured.[1]

While the Old Testament was originally written in Hebrew, it was later translated into Greek for use by Greek-speaking Jews. This transla-

---

1. G. Bonner, "Abortion and Early Christian Thought." in *Abortion and the Sanctity of Human Life*. Ed. by J. H. Channer (Exeter, UK: Paternoster Ltd., 1985), 101.

tion, also known as the *Septuagint*, contains an incorrect translation of the Hebrew version of Exodus 21:22–25. It states that if the miscarried child was "imperfectly formed" a fine would be due, but if the child was "perfectly formed" the violator deserved punishment by execution.[2] In other words, in the Greek text causing an early-term miscarriage was punishable by fine, while causing a later-term miscarriage was punishable by death.

One might wonder at this point how to define an "imperfectly formed" or "perfectly formed" child in regard to Exodus 21. This is an important question since the distinctions between 'formed' and 'unformed,' and 'souled' and 'unsouled' fetuses are discussed throughout this book. While the answer over the years has varied, one popular belief before the nineteenth century was that a fetus took the shape of a baby around 40 days gestation, at which time it was also ensouled. However, since we know today that the development of a child is continuous from the moment of conception (with a measurable heartbeat at only 20–30 days gestation), these distinctions are scientifically outdated and arbitrary.

The Greek text's distinction of punishments in Exodus 21 has often been mentioned by pro-choice biblical commentators, because they believe it indicates that an early-term abortion is not the equivalent of murder and should be permissible. But using this text to make a biblical case for the permissibility of an early-term abortion is flawed on two counts. First of all, the Greek version is *not* the original text and therefore can provide little biblical guidance on the matter. Secondly, even if it were reliable, it can only be said that it simply provides a lighter penalty for causing an earlier-term miscarriage (probably before 40 days gestation). The bottom line is that in all cases described above, both in the Greek and Hebrew versions, Exodus 21 shows that causing a miscarriage at any point in a pregnancy was considered sinful and was punishable under ancient Jewish law.

Any confusion over Exodus 21 can also be explained by reviewing the moral traditions of the Jewish people. These traditions amply demonstrate the high regard that biblical Judaism had for life growing within the womb. Ronald B. Bagnall, the former editor of *Lutheran Forum*, notes that the great cultural difference between the Jewish people and their Gentile neighbors was their respect for human life. He writes, "In contrast

---

2. Bonner, 101.

to other nomadic peoples, the Israelites were not allowed to leave behind those who had become a burden or a bother."[3] This care for human beings living outside the womb was also provided to those humans still living *inside* the womb. Michael Gorman, dean of the *Ecumenical Institute of Theology*, writes in his book *Abortion and the Early Church* that, "It was a given of Jewish thought and life that abortion, like exposure, was unacceptable, and this was well known in the ancient world."[4]

The historical Jewish belief in the sinfulness of abortion has also been well documented in its religious literature. For instance, the *Sibylline Oracles*, which were Jewish apocalyptic writings from the first and second century B.C., describe the sins of women who were condemned to hell. These women, "having burdens in the womb[,] produce[d] abortions; and their offspring [were] cast unlawfully away."[5] And in the *Sentences of Pseudo-Phocylides*, an example of Jewish wisdom literature that was written either in the first century B.C. or the first century A.D., states

> "A woman should not destroy the unborn babe in her belly."
>
> –Sentences of Pseudo-Phocylides

that "a woman should not destroy the unborn babe in her belly, nor after its birth throw it before the dogs and vultures as prey."[6] In addition, the apocryphal text 1 *Enoch*, which was written either in the first or second century B.C., reveals the negative attitude that the Jews had for abortion when it explains that a wicked angel taught human beings to "smash the embryo in the womb."[7]

Many contemporary scholars have also noted the strong pro-life beliefs of prominent Jewish thinkers, such as the philosopher Philo. For instance, Gorman has pointed out that Philo spoke out against abortion in the centuries before and during the time of Christ.[8] And G.

3. Ronald B. Bagnall, "*Lex Orandi, Lex Credendi*: Pro-Life Consistency and Distinctions," *Lutheran Forum*. vol. 32, no. 4, Winter 1998, 5.

4. Michael Gorman, *Abortion and the Early Church*. (Eugene OR: Wipf and Stock Publishers, 1998), 33–34.

5. Cited in ibid., 37.

6. Cited in Michael Gorman, "Why Is the New Testament Silent About Abortion?" *Christianity Today*. January 11, 1993, 27.

7. Cited in ibid., 28.

8. Michael Gorman, "Ahead to Our Past: Abortion and Christian Texts," *The Church*

Bonner, a former reader in theology at Durham University, concurs with Gorman's findings, and he even attributes Philo's position to his reliance upon Exodus 21:22–25.[9] In addition, the first-century Jewish historian Josephus, in his work *Against Apion*, recounts the prevailing law against abortion. He writes, "The law orders all the offspring to be brought up, and forbids women either to cause abortion or to make away with the foetus; a woman convicted of this is regarded as . . . [having committed] infanticide, because she destroys a soul and diminishes the race."[10]

The Roman historian Tacitus also comments on the strictness of Jewish abortion ethics in his book, *Historiae*. In this work, Tacitus wonders why the Jews would continue to have children after they had completed their wills and had assigned inheritances for their children, since the Romans would often abort or expose additional children after the family inheritance plan was completed.[11]

All of these examples amply demonstrate a high regard for unborn human life among Christianity's Jewish forbears. These beliefs had a deep influence on Sacred Scripture and on the practices of the early Christian church.

---

and Abortion, ed. by Paul T. Stallsworth (Nashville: Abingdon Press, 1993), 31.

9. Bonner, 93–94.

10. Gorman, *Abortion and the Early Church*, 43.

11. Noonan, John T. Jr., "An Almost Absolute Value in History," in *The Morality of Abortion: Legal and Historical Perspectives*, ed. by John T. Noonan Jr. (Cambridge, MA: Harvard University Press, 1970), 5.

2

In God's Own Words

The Biblical Pro-Life Message

THIS CHAPTER WILL TAKE a close look at the Scripture verses which shed light on the abortion question. The reader may want to compare the passages that will be presented in this chapter with the questionable biblical interpretations that are espoused by the pro-choice *Religious Coalition for Reproductive Choice* and its allies in chapter 6.

Many biblical commentators point out that the word "abortion" is never mentioned in Holy Scripture. While this is true, there are many verses within the Bible that touch indirectly upon the issue of abortion. The best example of an indirect reference is the Bible's prohibition of *pharmakeia.*

This word has been rendered in some Bible translations as "sorcery," or "magic arts." But John T. Noonan, editor of *The Morality of Abortion: Legal and Historical Perspectives*, and currently a Senior Circuit Judge on the U.S. Court of Appeals for the 9th Circuit, translates this word as the "manufacture of medicines," and references four verses in the books of Galatians and Revelation which contain this sin.[1] The first verse is Galatians 5:20, which references the sinful deeds of "idolatry and witch-craft [*pharmakeia*]; hatred, discord, jealousy, fits of rage, selfish ambition, dissensions, [and] factions." The second two references are Revelation 9:21 and 21:8, and they speak of the unrepentant attitude of those condemned to hell, "Nor did they repent of their murders, their magic arts [*pharmakon*], their sexual immorality or their thefts"; and, "But the cowardly,

---

1. Noonan, 8–9.

the unbelieving, the vile, the murderers, the sexually immoral, those who practice magic arts [*pharmakois*], the idolaters and all liars—their place will be in the fiery lake of burning sulfur." The last is Revelation 22:15, another reference to those individuals who have been condemned to hell. It states, "Outside are the dogs, those who practice magic arts [*pharmakoi*], the sexually immoral, the murderers, the idolaters and everyone who loves and practices falsehood." Notice that in all of the last three references, *pharmakois* ("magic arts" as the NIV renders the term) is found near the sins of sexual immorality and murder. Considering the categorization of the sin of *pharmakois* in these verses and the fact that the term also referred to the creation of medicines, many commentators, including Noonan, believe that some of the "medicines" that sorcerers created in biblical times were abortive draughts.[2]

Alvin Schmidt, a former professor of sociology at Illinois College and writer of the 2001 book *Under the Influence: How Christianity Transformed Civilization*, holds similar views on the term *pharmakeia*. He believes that it is best translated as the "the making and administering of potions," and he also asserts that other first and second-century documents support the theory that the word was used to describe abortifacients, as well as other types of potions.[3] He writes,

> That *pharmakeia* (*pharmakon*), as used by St. Paul in his letter to the Galatians and St. John in the book of Revelation, apparently refers to the practice of abortion has added support in extrabiblical literature, both pagan and Christian. Plutarch (A.D. 46–120), a pagan, uses *pharmakeia* to note that it was especially used for contraception and abortion purposes (Romulus 22 of his *Parallel Lives*). An early Christian document, the *Didache*, says that abortion is forbidden, and in so arguing, it uses the words *ou pharmakeuseis* (you shall not use potions). These words are immediately followed by "*ou phoneuseis teknon en phthora*" (you shall not kill a child by abortion). Thus, this passage seems to link potions (drugs) with the killing of an unborn child. Clement of Alexandria (155–215), an early influential church father, identifies *pharmakeia* as an abortifacient. In criticizing women who conceal

---

2. Noonan, 8–9.

3. Alvin Schmidt, *Under the Influence*. (Grand Rapids, MI: Zondervan Publishing House, 2001), 57–58.

their sexual sin, he links abortion (*phthora*) with the taking of potions (*pharmakois*).[4]

So it seems a compelling argument that a biblical prohibition of "magic arts" included a prohibition of abortion as well. Gorman, in his book *Abortion and the Early Church*, further verifies this theory by explaining that one of the sorcerer's responsibilities was the manufacture of abortifacients.[5]

The biblical message on abortion can also be seen in the Old Testament. The Orthodox Christian theologian, John Breck, has pointed out God's intimate involvement in the creation of the prophet Isaiah in the womb.[6] This active divine role is specifically demonstrated in Isaiah 49:1 and 5, which states, ". . . Before I was born the Lord called me; from

> Did you not pour me out like milk and curdle me like cheese, clothe me with skin and flesh and knit me together with bone and sinews?
>
> –Job 10:10–11

my birth he has made mention of my name . . . he who formed me in the womb to be his servant to bring Jacob back to him . . ." God's "hands on" effort can also be seen in Isaiah 44:2, which states, "This is what the Lord says—he who made you, who formed you in the womb . . ."

There are many other Old Testament passages which demonstrate the value of life in the womb. In Jeremiah 1:5, God said to the prophet, "Before I formed you in the womb I knew you, before you were born I set you apart; I appointed you as a prophet to the nations." God had a special plan for Jeremiah as a prophet to Israel and formed him in the womb for His special purpose. Since God has a plan for all human lives, it only makes sense that He purposely formed each person (like Jeremiah) in his mother's womb. Therefore, Scripture testifies to the principle that a person should not attempt to undo what God has lovingly completed.

While it is possible to see the Jeremiah and Isaiah passages as linked only to the prophetic vocation, a look at Psalm 139:13–16 should clearly

4. Schmidt, 57–58.

5. Michael Gorman, *Abortion and the Early Church*, 37.

6. John Breck, *The Sacred Gift of Life: Orthodox Christianity and Bioethics*. (Crestwood, NY: St. Vladimir's Press, 1998), 148.

dispel this notion. In that psalm, David, who did not have a prophetic call from God, praises God's handiwork in forming him.[7] He writes,

> For you created my inmost being; you knit me together in my mother's womb. I praise you because I am fearfully and wonderfully made; your works are wonderful, I know that full well. My frame was not hidden from you when I was made in the secret place. When I was woven together in the depths of the earth, your eyes saw my unformed body. All the days ordained for me were written in your book before one of them came to be.

Job is another biblical book that touches on the active role that God has in forming each person in the womb. In chapter 10:8–12, Job challenges God's decision to allow Satan to torment him, and in doing so, describes how God formed him in his mother's womb,

> Your hands shaped me and made me. Will you now turn and destroy me? Remember that you molded me like clay. Will you now turn me to dust again? Did you not pour me out like milk and curdle me like cheese, clothe me with skin and flesh and knit me together with bone and sinews? You gave me life and showed me your kindness, and in your providence watched over my spirit.

In this beautiful verse, just as in the Psalms 139 verse, God is intimately involved in an unborn child's development. Additionally, Job, as a formless child being created in his mother's womb, is shown as having the same personhood as a fully developed adult.

The references to the sanctity of human life in the womb are not limited to the Old Testament. In Luke 1:42–44, Mary's cousin Elizabeth exclaims, "Blessed are you among women, and blessed is the child you will bear! But why am I so favored, that the mother of my Lord should come to me? As soon as the sound of your greeting reached my ears, the baby in my womb leaped for joy." Interestingly, this verse actually has a "double" pro-life message since John the Baptist (the unborn child in Elizabeth's womb) leaps for joy at being in the presence of his Lord Jesus—another unborn child! This verse's pro-life message is truly hard to miss.

This chapter has shown that there are many verses in Holy Scripture which demonstrate a high regard for human life. From these verses, an overall pro-life worldview is easily recognized. Indeed, God's love for life is a consistent theme. The Bible shows that God plans the lives of men

---

7. Michael Gorman, e-mail interview with the author, January 2, 2008.

before they are born. He then creates life and nurtures it in the womb. God then sustains and protects the human beings that He has created. The Bible also prohibits the work of sorcerers, who were known to create potions which induced abortions. All of these facts lead to a unified pro-life perspective within scripture: a perspective, as Gorman has pointed out, where abortion has no place.[8] The next chapter will take a look at the writings of the early Christian church to see if these works continued the Bible's pro-life perspective.

8. Michael Gorman, e-mail interview with the author, August 12, 2007.

3

From Day One

Early Christian Views on Abortion

FROM ITS BEGINNINGS, THE Christian church has taught that abortion is immoral.[1] In the first-century church, a work was written which explained the teachings and morals of the apostles. This document, called the *Didache*, which we already mentioned in our discussion of *pharmakeia*, means "teaching" in Greek. It states,

> There are two paths; the one of life and one of death, and the difference between the two paths is great. This then is the path of life. First love the God who made you, and second, your neighbor as yourself. And whatever you do not want to happen to you, do not do to another . . . Do not murder, do not commit adultery, do not engage in pederasty, do not engage in sexual immorality. Do not steal, do not practice magic, do not use enchanted potions, do not abort a fetus or kill a child that is born . . .[2]

As explained in chapter 2 about the book of Revelation, in the *Didache* similar sins are categorized together. Therefore, one can learn a great deal about early church attitudes on abortion by reviewing the sins that were placed near it in the document. Since an aborted pregnancy was often the end result of fornication or adulterous relationships, it makes sense that these sexual sins were categorized near the sin of abortion. But also notice

---

1. Bernard J Ficarra, *Abortion Analyzed.* (Old Town, ME: Health Educator Publications, Inc., 1989), 114.

2. "Didache," in *Lost Scriptures: Books that Did Not Make It into the New Testament.* Ed. by Bart D. Ehrman, (New York: Oxford University Press, 2003), 212–13.

that abortion was found alongside murder and infanticide, and with the practice of magic and the use of enchanting potions.

Clearly, two things can be learned from these "sister sins." The first is that abortion was viewed as a sin that involved killing, and thus was categorized with murder and infanticide. And the second was that abortion, during the time of the early church, was related to the practice of magic and the use of enchanting potions.

Another first-century document, the *Epistle of Barnabas*, includes this commandment: "Thou shalt not slay the child by procuring abortion; nor, again, shalt thou destroy it after it is born."[3] Gorman points out that neither the *Didache* nor the *Epistle of Barnabas* made a distinction regarding the age of the fetus, or whether it was "formed" or "unformed." Rather, both writings included all unborn children in the prohibition.[4]

Another early Christian writing, called the *Apocalypse of Peter*, which was held by second-century theologian Clement of Alexandria to be a text which belonged in the Bible—also explicitly prohibits abortion. In this work's description of hell, it states,

> And near that place I saw another gorge in which the discharge and excrement of the tortured ran down and became like a lake. And there sat women, and the discharge came up to their throats; and opposite them sat many children, who were born prematurely weeping. And from them went forth rays of fire and smote the woman on the eyes. And these were those who produced children outside of marriage and who procured abortions.[5]

However, for those who are legitimately concerned with the singling out of women in this text, they can rest easy since the text later emphasized the punishment of both unrepentant mothers *and* fathers over the sin of abortion by stating that, "those [men and women] who slew them will be tortured forever."[6]

Clement followed the *Apocalypse of Peter*'s moral teachings by writing in his book *The Tutor*, "Our whole life can go on in observation of the laws of nature, if we gain dominion over our desires from the beginning

3. "The Epistle of Barnabas," in *The Early Church Fathers on CD-ROM.* (Salem OR: Harmony Media Inc., 2000).

4. Gorman, *Abortion and the Early Church*, 50.

5. Cited in ibid., 51.

6. Ibid., 51.

and if we do not kill, by various means of perverse art, the human off-spring, born according to the designs of divine providence; for these women who, in order to hide their immorality, use abortive drugs which expel the matter completely dead, abort at the same time their human feelings."[7] What is so powerful about this quote is not only Clement's recognition of the sinfulness of abortion, but also his understanding of the psychological damage it inflicts on the women who have experienced it. The quote also demonstrates that little has changed since Clement's day, with the devastating emotional effects of abortion being as widespread today as they were 18 centuries ago.

Athenagoras, a second-century Christian apologist, was one of a number of early writers who defended the faith against the spurious accusation that it endorsed cannibalism. This belief among the Romans came from a false understanding regarding the Christian sacrament of Holy Communion. The argument went that since Christians ate the "body and blood" of Christ during the sacrament, they must somehow be cannibals. In an attempt to debunk this myth, Athenagoras writes in his *A Plea for the Christians*, "What reason would we have to commit murder when we say that women who induce abortions are murderers, and will have to give account of it to God."[8] He also writes, "For the fetus in the womb is not an animal, and it is God's providence that he exist."[9] In other words, Christians had a much stricter definition of murder than did the pagans—since it included abortion and infanticide—so it did not make sense that such a religion would advocate cannibalism.

> "These women who, in order to hide their im-morality, use abortive drugs which expel the matter completely dead, abort at the same time their human feelings."
>
> –Clement of Alexandria

Another apologetic text called the *Epistle to Diognetus*, written in the second or third century by an anonymous Christian, speaks of the high esteem that Christians had for unborn children, in contrast to the rest of

7. Cited in Gorman, *Abortion and the Early Church*, 52–53.

8. Cited in ibid., 54.

9. Cited in John Riddle, *Eve's Herbs*. (Cambridge, MA: Harvard University Press, 1998), 83.

Roman society. It states that "They [Christians] marry as do all others; they beget children, but they do not destroy their offspring."[10]

The defense of Christianity against charges of cannibalism continued in the third century with writers such as Minucius Felix. Minucius, in his apologetic work *Octavius,* reveals the pro-life views of Christianity when he points out that it was the Romans who were the murderers, not the Christians, and uses abortion as an example. He writes, "There are [non-Christian] women who [are] committing infanticide before they give birth to the infant."[11] He also writes in *Octavius* that "the story about Christians drinking the blood of an infant that they have murdered [another example of a misunderstanding by the pagans concerning Holy Communion], is a barefaced calumny. But the Gentiles, both cruelly expose their children newly born, and before they are born destroy them by a cruel abortion."[12]

Tertullian, the famous attorney and African Church Father, wrote his *Apology* (197 A.D.) to defend the Christian faith against false allegations that it sacrificed infants during its religious services. In the work, he explains that Christians would not even procure abortions, much less sacrifice a child already born. He writes,

> But for us [Christians], to whom homicide has been once for all forbidden, it is not permitted to break up even what has been conceived in the womb, while the blood is still being drawn from the mother's body to make a new creature. Prevention of birth is premature murder; and it makes no difference whether it is a life already born that one snatches away or a life that is coming to birth that one destroys. The future man is a man already: the whole fruit is present in the seed.[13]

Thus Tertullian uses the "whole fruit is present in the seed" analogy to demonstrate the full humanity of the fetus within the womb of the mother.

Tertullian also believed that a child received its soul (and thus its life) at the moment of conception. As mentioned before, the timing of when an unborn child was infused with a soul was actively debated among

---

10. George W. Grube, ed. *What the Church Fathers Say About . . .* , vols. 1 and 2. (Minneapolis, MN: Light and Life Publishing Co., 2005), 148.

11. Gorman, "Ahead to Our Past: Abortion and Christian Texts," 34.

12. Minucius Felix "The Octavius," in *The Early Church Fathers on CD-ROM.* (Salem OR: Harmony Media Inc., 2000).

13. Cited in Bonner, 93–94.

Christian theologians during the third century. In defending his view that the soul was infused (and therefore life began) at the beginning of a pregnancy, Tertullian wrote, "we acknowledge, therefore, that life begins with conception, because we contend that the soul begins at conception. Life begins when the soul begins."[14]

Yet Tertullian also reluctantly recognized the need to allow abortions in those rare cases when it was the only means to save the mother's life during a difficult childbirth. Tertullian referred to the killing of the child in these cases as a "necessary cruelty."[15]

Cyprian, the third-century Bishop of Carthage and great defender of the church against the numerous heretical movements of his day, utilized the term "parricide" (the killing of a close relative) to describe abortion. And he also used the story of a schismatic bishop who kicked his pregnant wife in order to make her to miscarry, as an example of the sinfulness of those who left the church.[16] In doing so, he inadvertently reaffirmed the church's prohibition on abortion.

The influence that these early Christian writers had on Roman society was profound. In fact, some scholars believe that the writings of Tertullian, Athenagoras, and others, led to the institution of numerous anti-abortion restrictions by Roman authorities in the third century.[17]

By the fourth century, Christian councils began to proscribe church punishments for those who had procured abortions. At the Synod of Elvira (Spain) in 305, the synod condemned the sin of abortion, and it excommunicated those who procured abortions. In addition, the penance was severe: allowing reentry into the church for these transgressors only at their deathbeds.[18] In 314, the Council of Ancyra (then the capital of Galatia and today the capital of Turkey—Ankara[19]) followed suit but with a shorter penance, restricting post-abortive women from participating in the sacraments of communion or baptism for a penitential period of ten years.[20] The council's canon states, "Concerning women who com-

14. Cited in Grube, 150.

15. Bonner, 99.

16. John Connery, *Abortion: The Development of the Roman Catholic Perspective.* (New Orleans: Loyola University Press, 1977), 44.

17. Gorman, *Abortion and the Early Church*, 62.

18. Schmidt, 58.

19. Bonner, 107.

20. Gorman, *Abortion and the Early Church*, 65.

mit fornication, and destroy that which they have conceived, or who are employed in making drugs for abortion, a former decree excluded them until the hour of death, and to this some have assented. Nevertheless, being desirous to use somewhat greater lenity, we have ordained that they fulfill ten years [of penance], according to the prescribed degrees . . . Harlots taking injurious medicines are to be subjected to penance for ten years."[21]

While the time periods for abortion penances were proscribed by canon law, the specific punishments were usually left to the discretion of the penitent's confessor. For instance, under the canon law of Ancyra, a woman who confessed the sin of abortion would be excluded from receiving communion for a period of ten years, with additional requirements assigned at the discretion of her priest. These specifics might include the abstention from meat, the recitation of certain prayers, or the requirement to complete a pilgrimage to a holy site.

Also in the fourth century, Ambrose, the great Bishop of Milan and mentor of Augustine, spoke out against abortions which were motivated by the desire to maximize the inheritance of one's children. He wrote, "The wealthy, in order that their inheritance may not be divided among several, deny in the very womb their own progeny. By use of parricidal mixtures they snuff out the fruit of their wombs in the genital organs themselves. In this way life is taken away before it is given . . . Who except man himself has taught us ways of repudiating children?"[22]

Zeno, the Bishop of Verona from 362–380, also spoke out on the practice, suggesting that greed often led parents to procure abortion. He explained that abortion was often performed in his day to save the expense of raising an additional child, or (as Ambrose had discussed) to save an inheritance for someone else.[23] One cannot fail to see how little has changed since Zeno's day regarding the monetary motivations for abortion.

The consistent anti-abortion position of the fourth-century church can also be seen in the writings of the famed theologian John Chrysostom. John was the patriarch of Constantinople and his mass liturgy is still celebrated in many Eastern Orthodox churches. In discussing the termination of a pregnancy which resulted from an affair with a prostitute, he wrote,

21. "The Canons of the Council of Ancyra," in *The Early Church Fathers on CD-ROM*. (Salem OR: Harmony Media Inc., 2000).

22. Cited in Gorman, *Abortion and the Early Church*, 68.

23. Ibid., 52.

> Why sow where the ground makes it its care to destroy the fruit? where there are many efforts at abortion? where there is murder before the birth? for even the harlot thou dost not let continue a mere harlot, but makest her a murderess also. You see how drunkenness leads to whoredom, whoredom to adultery, adultery to murder; or rather to a something even worse than murder. For I have no name to give it, since it does not take off the thing born, but prevents its being born. Why then dost thou abuse the gift of God, and fight with His laws, and follow after what is a curse as if a blessing, and make the chamber of procreation a chamber for murder, and arm the woman that was given for childbearing unto slaughter?[24]

By the end of that century, the theology of a fetal soul was expressed in the Christian document *Apostolic Constitutions*, and in that work abortion was seen to destroy the life of an ensouled human being.[25] Interestingly, this prohibition on abortion also followed a number of warnings against witchcraft, once again linking the practice of sorcery with the abortion trade.[26]

Augustine (354–430), the famed Bishop of Hippo and writer of *Confessions* and *City of God*, wrote about abortion as well, and in his writings he made a legal distinction between "formed" and "unformed" fetuses, as had some other Christians before him who relied on the Greek translation of Exodus 21. He also advocated stricter penalties for those who aborted a child at a later phase of gestation.[27]

Many pro-choice commentators such as Daniel Dombrowski and Robert Deltete in their book, *Brief, Liberal, Catholic Defense of Abortion*, have used this opinion of Augustine's to make the case that the Bishop of Hippo would have approved of the legality of any first trimester abortion. They have categorized Augustine's view of the conceptus as that of a mere a seed which needs to develop in order to become life.[28]

But Deltete and Dombrowski have incorrectly equated Augustine's views on the *penalties due* for abortion at various phases of fetal develop-

---

24. St. John Chrysostom, "Commentary on the Epistle of St Paul to the Romans," in *The Early Church Fathers on CD-ROM*. (Salem OR: Harmony Media Inc. 2000).

25. "Constitutions of the Holy Apostles," in *The Early Church Fathers on CD-ROM*. (Salem OR: Harmony Media Inc., 2000).

26. Ibid.

27. Anne Hendershott, *The Politics of Abortion*. (New York: Encounter Books, 2006), 96.

28. Ibid., 96.

ment with his views on the *sinfulness* of abortion. While the Christian faith (before the 1960s) has occasionally made a distinction in the *penalties* for late or early-term abortions, it has nevertheless consistently considered almost all abortions to be sinful acts. The clear words of Augustine in his treatise *On Marriage and Concupiscence* (ca. 420) are instructive here, since they show his total disgust for the types of sexual relationships that often result in abortion:

> Sometimes (*Aliquando*) this lustful cruelty or cruel lust goes so far as to employ drugs to cause sterility; and if this is ineffective it finds a way to destroy and expel fetuses conceived in the womb, willing its offspring to die before it lives [if the fetus is unformed] or, if it is already quickened in the womb [i.e. if it is already formed], to die before it is born. Very well then: if both parties are such [as to do this], they are not married; and if they were such from the beginning, they have come together not by wedlock but rather by debauchery. If however they are not both such, I make bold to say that either the woman is in some way the husband's harlot or the man the wife's adulterer.[29]

And notice that regardless of whether Augustine is speaking of "unformed" or "formed" unborn children, he still states that all abortions are sinful because they kill one's offspring. He also points out that abortion destroys the marital covenant, making the married couple no better than adulterers and prostitutes.

It is also important to understand that the church was by no means unanimous in its view that early abortions should receive lesser penances than later-term abortions. The church father Basil of Caesarea wrote in his *Epistle to Amphilochius* that, "[a] woman . . . is a murderer . . . who take[s] medicines to procure abortion," and in the same letter, also made the penalty for an abortion—regardless of the length of the child's gestation—ten years of penance."[30] He states, "Let her that procures abortion undergo ten years penance, *whether the embryo were perfectly formed, or not* [italics added]."[31]

29. Cited in Bonner, 109.

30. St. Basil, "First Canonical Epistle to Amphilochius," in *The Early Church Fathers on CD-ROM*. (Salem OR: Harmony Media Inc., 2000).

31. Ibid.

Basil also worked to assist women who found themselves in unplanned pregnancies.[32] And he petitioned Emperor Valentinian to ban the guild of sorcerers (the *sagae*) which performed abortions. These early abortionists were especially notorious, since they reportedly sold the bodies of aborted infants to the makers of cosmetic creams.[33]

Basil's steadfast efforts were rewarded when the emperor ordered the prohibition of abortion in 374.[34] Basil's brother, Gregory, the Bishop of Nyssa, was also strongly pro-life, and he also viewed abortion as murder from the moment of conception.[35]

Another great early church advocate of the unborn was Jerome (340–420), who is probably best known for writing the first translation of the Bible into Latin. He explained that "some [women], when they learn that they are with child through sin, practice abortion by the use of drugs. Frequently they die themselves and are brought before the rulers of the lower world guilty of three crimes: suicide, adultery against Christ, and murder of an unborn child."[36] Jerome actually warned of certain "root poisons" which were the abortifacients of his day, and which John Riddle, a history professor at North Carolina State University, believes were the herbs barrenwort and birthwort.[37]

Now that the early church's pro-life stance on abortion has been amply demonstrated, the next chapter will review the opinions of the medieval councils and theologians to see if they remained consistent with the early years of Christianity.

32. Schmidt, 59.

33. Ibid., 59.

34. Ibid., 59.

35. Daniel M. Dombrowski and Robert J. Deltete, *A Brief, Liberal, Catholic Defense of Abortion.* (Urbanna, IL: University of Illinois Press, 2000), 27–28.

36. Gorman, *Abortion and the Early Church*, 68.

37. John M. Riddle, *Contraception and Abortion from the Ancient World to the Rennaissance.* (Cambridge, MA: Harvard University Press, 1992), 43–45.

4

Penalties and Penance

Christian Views on Abortion in the Middle Ages

THE MIDDLE AGES (500–1500 A.D.) was also a period of consistent pro-life opinion within the Christian church. For instance, Caesarius, the Bishop of Arles (France) from 503–543, spoke out against those who would ingest "potions for purposes of abortion."[1] Local church councils also consistently condemned the practice. In 524, the Council of Lerida (Spain), pronounced that an adulterer who procured an abortion, whether male or female, would be required to serve seven years of penance before being received back into the church, while an individual who made the poisons could only be received back into the church on his or her death-bed. Lerida also pronounced that any clergyman involved in such a sin would receive the same penances as those above, and would also lose his ministry position.[2] The Council of Braga (572), in what is today Portugal, also pronounced a similar penance of seven years for those involved in abortion.[3]

A few years later, in 580, John the Faster, the patriarch of Constantinople, also wrote a canon against abortion. It states, "As for women who destroy embryos professionally, and those who give or take poisons with the object of aborting babies and dropping them prematurely, we

---

1. Riddle, *Contraception and Abortion from the Ancient World to the Rennaissance*, 111.

2. Connery, 60.

3. Ibid., 61.

prescribed the rule that they be treated as public penitents."[4] Furthermore, the patriarch also recommended that the penance was to last from three to five years.[5]

As shown in the previous two chapters, the practice of abortion was often linked to witchcraft. For instance, Columban (559–615), the famous Irish monastic, likened the use of abortifacients to sorcery, as had the biblical and early church writers, and he warned against those who "destroyed someone [committed abortion] by his 'magic art' [*maleficio*]."[6]

Although abortion was seen as sinful throughout all nine months of pregnancy, just as in the early church period there was some debate among medieval theologians as to when a fetus was ensouled. However, Maximus the Confessor (580–662), like Tertullian, held strongly in his treatise *Ambiguorum liber*, that a child's soul was infused from the moment of conception, and for that reason abortion was to be considered murder at any stage of pregnancy.[7]

Later, the Synod of Trullo, a meeting of church leaders held in Constantinople in 692, pronounced that "those who give drugs for procuring abortion, and those who receive poisons to kill the foetus, are subjected to the penalty of murder." And "whoever gives or receives medicine to produce abortion is [guilty of] a homicide."[8] While today it may seem unjust to punish those who have had abortions with similar penalties as those who commit murder against those already born, this view was not uncommon in the Middle Ages, and it demonstrates the medieval church's high regard for developing human life within the womb.

The witness in Ireland against abortion was strong during the Middles Ages, as it remains today. The *Canones Hibernenses*, which were written circa 675, were Irish canons that provided for a penance of three and one-half years for an early-term abortion, and seven years for a late-term abortion.[9]

---

4. Grube, 149.

5. Ibid., 149.

6. Riddle, *Contraception and Abortion from the Ancient World to the Rennaissance*, 110.

7. Connery, 51.

8. "The Canons of the Council in Trullo," in *The Early Church Fathers on CD-ROM*. (Salem OR: Harmony Media Inc., 2000).

9. Connery, 68.

Collections of canons which were gathered from numerous councils also circulated throughout the Middle Ages, and were called *prisca* or *itala*. One of these *prisca* called the *Dionysius Exiguus*, was endorsed by Pope Hadrian I, who reigned from 772–795. It included the Ancyra canons against abortion, and was used by the Emperor Charlemagne and other medieval rulers for the next two centuries.[10]

One of the most knowledgeable scholars on abortion during the Middle Ages was the late John Connery, a former professor of moral theology at Loyola University. Connery noted that the Middle Ages were replete with confessional booklets that were written as guides for priests in hearing confessions. The vast majority of these guides dealt with the sinfulness of abortion, and they were attributed to such famous Christian saints as Columban, Bede, Finnian, and others.[11] An example of such a guide is the *Capitulare*, written by Theodulph Halitigar (d. 824), the Bishop of Orleans. In that work, he proscribed a seven-year penance for a woman who had an abortion.[12]

Similar penitential sentences could also be found in medieval Germany. At the Council of Mainz in 847, the fathers of the council repeated the decrees against abortion that were pronounced at the councils of Ancyra, Lerida, and Elvira.[13] And, in 848, the Council of Worms stated that those who had procured abortions had, in fact, committed murder. This council was especially noteworthy in that it was the first local council which equated an abortion with murder.[14] In 906, Regino the abbot of Prum, Germany, also provided penance guidelines for abortions, from one year for an early-term abortion and increasing in severity for later-term abortions.[15] Burchard, the Bishop of Worms, who wrote his *Decretum* sometime between 1012 and 1022, suggested a penance of three years for all abortions, regardless of how late they occurred in the pregnancy.[16]

Ivo, the Bishop of Chartes (in France) from 1040–1116, also held that abortion was sinful from the moment of conception. Riddle sums

10. Connery, 62.

11. Ibid., 72–73.

12. Ibid., 78.

13. Ibid., 79.

14. Ibid., 80.

15. Ibid., 80.

16. Ibid., 82.

up Ivo's view nicely when he writes, "God, not herbs, should decide who is born. In Ivo's position, abortion was not wrong after the fetus formed, it was wrong period. It was *contra naturum* [against nature]."[17] Ivo's view was later included in Peter Lombard's theology, and in his famous book, the *Sentences,* which became the standard theological text used in medieval seminaries.[18]

Another theologian who was deeply influenced by Ivo was Gratian, a Camaldolese monk from Bologna, who is recognized within Christianity as being the father of canon law.[19] Gratian wrote his *Concordia canonum discordantium* in the twelfth century in order to consolidate the many canons which were in circulation at the time. This work, which also provided penances for abortion, became known as the *Decretum Gratiani.*[20]

> God, not herbs, should decide who is born. In Ivo's position, abortion was not wrong after the fetus formed, it was wrong period. It was *contra naturum* [against nature].
>
> –John Riddle

And Bernard, the Bishop of Pavia in Italy (d. 1213), who compiled his own list of canons, also followed Ivo's precedent of placing the subject of abortion under the heading *Homicidio.*[21] Later in the century, Pope Gregory IX's (1227–1241) *Decretals,* purported to be the first listing of canon laws that governed the entire church, stated that an abortion performed at any stage of gestation was considered to be murder.[22] And although Thomas Aquinas (1225–1274), the great Dominican theologian and philosopher did not believe that an unborn child was ensouled until 40 days (for boys) and 80 days (for girls) of gestation, he nevertheless viewed abortion as a clearly sinful act at any time during a woman's pregnancy.[23]

---

17. John Riddle, *Eve's Herbs.* (Cambridge, MA: Harvard University Press, 1998), 93.

18. Ibid., 93.

19. Ibid., 93.

20. Connery, 82.

21. Ibid., 96.

22. Susan T. Nicholson, *Abortion and the Roman Catholic Church.* (Notre Dame, IN: Religious Ethics, Inc., 1978), 14.

23. Hendershott, 96.

In 1398, for the first time, canon law stated that abortion immediately excommunicated the offender.[24] And the relationship between those who practiced sorcery and performed abortions was shown to last even throughout the fifteenth century, since Pope Innocent VIII, in his bull (edict letter) against witchcraft, *Summis desiderantes* (1484), also prohibited abortions performed by witches.[25]

As mentioned before, the centuries of the Middle Ages produced numerous books which guided priests in providing penances during the sacrament of confession. According to Connery, the fifteenth century showed an explosion in the number of these guides, also called *summae*. All of these guides instructed priests on the required penances for abortions at various stages of pregnancy, and even gave instruction on how to deal with monks who entered into sexual relationships and then tried to cover up those liaisons through procured abortion.[26] It was John of Naples' *Summa* which first gained some acceptance for the morality of therapeutic abortions which were performed (before the quickening of the fetus) to save the life of the mother. However, this exception to the prohibition on abortion was never universally held within the church.[27]

The descriptions shown above demonstrate that there were some differences of opinion about the length of the penances that should be given to those involved in abortions. These debates also delved into the issue of whether a late-term abortion was more sinful than an early-term abortion. This debate led, in turn, to issues of when a fetus was 'ensouled,' when a child in the womb was 'formed,' and when the child was 'animated,' (what we now often call 'quickened,' or able to be felt moving within the womb by the mother).[28]

Pro-choice Christians often use such debates from the early church or the Middle Ages to suggest that the church allowed, or at least tolerated, early-term abortions. However, nothing could be further from the truth. Almost invariably, the medieval church considered abortions to be gravely immoral. These debates within medieval Christianity usually took place in order to answer the question of when an abortion could be

24. Kerry N. Jacoby, *Souls, Bodies, Spirits.* (Westport, CT: Praeger Publishers, 1998), 30.

25. Riddle, *Eve's Herbs*, 126.

26. Connery, 119–21.

27. Ibid., 124.

28. Ibid., 95.

considered murder under the civil law. Since the answer to this question could determine whether the parents or abortionists could be executed, it was an important question indeed, and worthy of discussion.[29]

Some of these debates were also based on the poor embryology of the time, and the belief that at a certain point a child changed from liquid into a baby. Due to the use of ultrasound today, such debate is unnecessary, since substantial development can be now seen in the growing fetus in the first few weeks of gestation.

The use of these medieval debates by pro-choice Christians also appears disingenuous, since their arguments would require them to believe, at the very least, that all non-therapeutic abortions after the first trimester were sinful. However, such an acknowledgement was found to be sorely lacking among Christian abortion proponents during the recent debate over partial-birth abortion.

The testimony of numerous church councils, canons, and theologians clearly shows that the medieval period was a time of doctrinal consistency on the immorality of abortion. Indeed, the sinfulness of abortion was consistently held during the entire one thousand year span of the Middle Ages. The next chapter will take a look at the Christian perspectives on abortion since the Reformation. This historical review will also take special interest in the Protestant Reformers to see if their views had any impact on those of pro-choice Christians today.

29. Connery, 100.

5

Great Minds

Views of Prominent Theologians Since the Reformation

I N CHAPTER 4, IT was shown that the early church's doctrine on the sinfulness of abortion continued throughout the Middle Ages. It was consistently espoused by the leaders of the Protestant Reformation as well.

The great Reformation leader Martin Luther had great respect for the sanctity of life in the womb. In a commentary on Genesis 25 (which speaks of Abraham and his numerous offspring), Luther explained how God's attitude towards children was often different from our own. The reformer taught that God did not view the newly conceived child as a burden, but rather recognized each child as a precious gift. Consequently, Luther saw abortion as a wicked destruction of God's plan of creation. He wrote, "He [God] is not hostile to children, as we are. But God emphasizes His word to such an extent that He sometimes gives offspring even to those who do not desire it, yes even hate it . . . *How great, therefore, the wickedness of human nature is! How many girls there are who prevent conception and kill and expel tender fetuses, although procreation is the work of God*" [italics added].[1]

John Calvin, the famous Reformation leader in sixteenth-century France and Switzerland, who is recognized today as the father of the Presbyterian and Reformed denominations, was also a strong defender of the sanctity of life within the womb. Calvin continued the long-standing position of the church on the sinfulness of abortion when he wrote,

1. Martin Luther, *Luther's Works* vol. 4. ed. by Jaroslav Pelikan and Helmut Lehmann (St. Louis: Concordia Publishing, 1964), 304.

the *foetus*, though enclosed in the womb of its mother, is already a human being (*homo*), and it is almost a monstrous crime to rob it of the life which it has not yet begun to enjoy. If it seems more horrible to kill a man in his own house than in a field, because a man's house is his place of most secure refuge, it ought surely to be deemed more atrocious to destroy a *foetus* in the womb before it has come to light . . .[2]

In the Roman Catholic Church, prominent leaders of the Counter-Reformation were also outspoken defenders of the unborn. Pope Sixtus V (the famous renaissance pope who completed the dome of St. Peter's), in his bull *Effraenatam* (1588) prohibited abortion "by means of magical deeds (*maleficiis*) and by cursed medicines (*maleficiis medicamentis*)."[3] According to Connery, *Effraenatam* was elicited by an escalation of the incidence of abortion in the sixteenth century.[4] In the bull, Sixtus V writes, "the most severe punishments [should go to those] who procure poisons to extinguish and destroy the conceived fetus within the womb."[5] According to Riddle, this prohibition also included those who even counseled a woman to have an abortion.[6] Because of the harshness of punishments—equivalent to those for murder—for any abortion after conception, *Effraenatam* was repealed and the previous canon law, which included more lenient sanctions, was reinstated by Pope Gregory XIV in 1591.[7]

In the seventeenth century, the Roman Catholic Church maintained its strong pro-life stance. In 1679, Pope Innocent XI condemned two misplaced views about abortion that were circulating through the writings of the Jesuit scholar Tomas Sanchez, professor of Moral Theology in Granada, Spain, and the writings of the theologian Juan Caramel y Lobkowicz.[8] The first view (held by Sanchez) was that abortion should be allowed until the unborn child was ensouled (usually assumed to occur at

---

2. John Calvin, *Commentaries on the Last Four Books of Moses.* (Grand Rapids, MI: Baker Books, 1993), 3:41–42.

3. Riddle, *Eve's Herbs*, 136.

4. Connery, 147.

5. Riddle, *Eve's Herbs*, 157.

6. Ibid., 158.

7. Noonan, 33.

8. Ibid., 33–34.

the fortieth day of gestation by canon law[9]), in order to avoid the threat of having a young mother killed or defamed for her dishonor.[10] The second view, held by Caramel y Lobkowicz, was that a child was not ensouled until birth, and therefore no abortion should be considered homicide.[11] Innocent made it clear that both these views were incorrect and inconsistent with previous Catholic doctrine and canon law.[12]

The pro-life witness of the Christian faith soon traveled across the Atlantic to the American colonies. John Wesley, who was the spiritual founder of today's Methodist denominations, and a leader of the First Great Awakening, always took a strong stand against the practice of abortion. He made a missionary journey to Georgia in 1736 and he kept a diary of his travels. The following journal account shows the disparity between the Indian ethical practices (which allowed abortion) and the morality of Christianity at the time.

> Thursday, July 1.—The Indians had an audience; and another on Saturday, when Chicali, their head man, dined with Mr. Oglethorpe [the colonial governor]. After dinner, I asked the grey-headed old man what he thought he was made for. He said, "He that is above knows what He made us for. We know nothing. We are in the dark. But white men know much. And yet white men build great houses, as if they were to live forever. But white men cannot live forever. In a little time, white men will be dust as well as I." I told him, "If red men will learn the Good Book, they may know as much as white men. But neither we nor you can understand that Book unless we are taught by Him that is above: and He will not teach you unless you avoid what you already know is not good." He answered, "I believe that. He will not teach us while our hearts are not white. And our men do what they know is not good: they kill their own children. *And our women do what they know is not good: they kill the child before it is born.* Therefore He that is above does not send us the Good Book. [italics added][13]

While this quote is undoubtedly dated regarding racial attitudes of whites towards Native Americans, it nevertheless shows that Wesley

---

9. Noonan, 47.

10. Ibid., 33–34.

11. Ibid., 33–34.

12. Riddle, *Eve's Herbs*, 158.

13. John Wesley, *Journal of John Wesley*. (Chicago: Moody Press, 1951), 21.

taught that abortion was sinful, and that he believed that it was a sin which hindered a proper understanding of God's Word.

In addition, while speaking about the immoral practices of some of the Indians he encountered in Georgia the following year, Wesley entered in his journal on December 30, 1737 that it was "a common thing for a son to shoot his father or mother because they are old and past labour, and *for a woman to either procure abortion*, or to throw her child into the next river, because she will go with her husband to the war." [italics added][14] Notice that he linked the sin of abortion to the killing of one's parents and also to the sin of infanticide. This statement from Wesley once again demonstrates Christianity's tendency to categorize abortion with other types of "killing" sins.

The nineteenth century was an important era in U.S. abortion history, since it resulted in the tightening of many abortion laws nationwide. This effort was led primarily by the medical community and by anti-vice activists like Andrew Comstock.

Janet Farrell Brodie, professor of history at Claremont Graduate University, in her book *Contraception and Abortion in Nineteenth Century America*, has stated that few clergy spoke out on the abortion problem at that time.[15] James C. Mohr, professor of history at the University of Oregon confirms this silence, especially during the period before the Civil War.[16]

Mohr gives three reasons for clergy inactivity on the issue. First, he asserts that the majority of clergymen believed that church-going women were not affected or involved with abortion. Second, he believes that many preachers thought that abortion before quickening could be seen as morally ambiguous by society at large. Third, Mohr concludes that many ministers believed that preaching on the sin of abortion would drive parishioners away from the pews.[17] This was partly due to the modesty of the era, which discouraged discussions about sexual topics. It also seems likely that the nineteenth-century churches had the luxury of staying

14. John Wesley, *Journal of John Wesley, AM.* ed. by Nehemiah Currock. (London: The Epworth Press, 1960), 1:407.

15. Janet Farrell Brodie, *Contraception and Abortion in Nineteenth Century America*. (Ithaca, NY: Cornell University Press, 1994), 153.

16. James C. Mohr, *Abortion in America: the Origins and Evolution of National Policy, 1800–1900.* (New York: Oxford University Press, 1978), 183–84.

17. Ibid., 185.

out of the debate, since secular organizations like the *American Medical Association* had already taken the lead in the fight against abortion.

While this reluctance to address the issue of abortion undoubtedly existed, just as it exists among many Christian clergymen and women today, it does not indicate a pro-choice opinion on behalf of the American clergy during that time. And, unlike today, there is no evidence of Christian clergy who were outspoken in their advocacy of abortion.

On the contrary, when abortion was addressed from the pulpit, the message was invariably pro-life. Even before the Civil War, Roman Catholic voices were clearly heard on the topic. For example, the Catholic Bishop of Boston, John Bernard Fitzpatrick, wrote in 1858 that abortion was a "sin so directly opposite to the first laws of nature, and to the designs of God, our Creator, that it cannot fail to draw down a curse upon the land where it is generally practiced."[18] Another staunch supporter of the pro-life movement was the *YMCA*, which gave early support to Andrew Comstock in his efforts to expose the elicit abortion trade.[19] While the *YMCA* is often seen these days as an athletic club, in the nineteenth century it was an active Christian ministry devoted to protecting young men from vice.

Although anti-abortion preaching was not occurring in every pulpit, it was not uncommon for religious denominations to become involved in anti-vice efforts during this time, with one of their ministries being the elimination of abortion. For instance, Comstock's pastor, William Ives Buddington, the pastor of a congregational church in Brooklyn, was a member of the *New York Society for the Suppression of Vice*.[20] Another anti-vice group was Philadelphia's *Citizen's Representative Committee*, whose leaders included "the bishops of the Protestant Episcopal and Reformed Episcopal churches, and ministers from the Presbyterian, Baptist, Methodist Episcopal, Lutheran, Dutch Reformed, German Reformed, Unitarian, and United Presbyterian churches."[21] A similar organization in Boston called the *Watch and Ward Society* was led by Frederick Baylies Allen, the assistant Episcopal minister of Trinity Church.[22]

18. Cited in Mohr, 186.

19. Nicola Beisel, *Imperiled Innocents: Anthony Comstock and Family Reproduction in Victorian America*. (Princeton: Princeton University Press, 1997), 38.

20. Brodie, 261.

21. Beisel, 137.

22. Brodie, 261.

The anti-abortion effort also garnered support from famed Indiana pastor, E. Frank Howe, who preached that, "Taking the life of the unborn child is a crime, and that crime is none other than murder."[23] Congregational minister Rev. John Todd was also outspokenly pro-life, writing in his 1867 book, *Serpents in the Dove's Nest* that abortion was "fashionable murder."[24] Todd also stated in an 1867 article in the *Congregationalist and Boston Recorder* that any abortion (even before quickening) was "deliberate cold murder."[25]

Mohr also documents an August 1868 statement against abortion by the Maine Conference of the Congregational Church which states, "Let imagination draw the darkest picture that reason or taste could allow, and it would fail to set forth adequately the outlines and shocking details of this practice," and "full one third of the natural population of our land fails by the hand of violence; that in no one year of the late war have so many lost life in camp or battle, as have failed of life by reason of this horrid home crime."[26]

The Presbyterian Church also spoke out on the subject in 1869. At that time, the denomination was separated into what was referred to as the "Old School" and the "New School." In preparation for the union of these two schools the following year, the "Old School" held a convention in New York City to vote on the merger.[27] The convention passed a pro-life overture offered by Rev. Robert Beer of northern Indiana, which stated, "This assembly regards the destruction by parents of their own offspring, before birth, with abhorrence, as a crime against God and against nature; and as the frequency of such murders can no longer be concealed, we hereby warn those that are guilty of this crime that, except they repent, they cannot inherit eternal life."[28]

Mohr also gives the example of Cleveland Coxe, the Episcopal Bishop of Western New York, who wrote in an 1869 pastoral letter that he had previously preached to his congregation about the "blood-guiltiness

---

23. Cited in Riddle, *Eve's Herbs*, 223.
24. Brodie, 153.
25. Mohr, 187–88.
26. Ibid., 188.
27. Ibid., 191.
28. Cited in ibid., 192.

of ante-natal infanticide."[29] He also referred to abortions as "crimes which ... [are] likened to the sacrifices of Moloch."[30] Coxe also published a book on the subject and addressed the clergy in his diocese on the sinfulness of abortion in March of that same year.[31] Also in 1869, the Catholic Bishop of Baltimore, Martin John Spaulding, condemned abortion in a pastoral letter to his diocese. In the letter, Spaulding states, "The murder of an infant before its birth is, in the sight of God and His Church, as great a crime, as would be the killing of a child after birth."[32]

The issue of abortion hit critical mass after an article was written by Augustus St. Clair in the August 23, 1871 *New York Times* that exposed the elicit abortion trade in New York City and called it the "evil of the age."[33] At that time, abortion services were subtly (and sometimes not so subtly) advertised in New York newspapers.[34] St. Clair visited many of these advertised clinics with a young woman who pretended to be pregnant and seeking abortion services.[35] Four days after his exposé appeared in the paper, news broke that a woman was found to have been killed by a botched abortion, and that her nude body was found in a trunk being shipped to Chicago.[36] St. Clair later realized that he had previously seen the deceased in an abortionist's waiting room just days before.[37] As the newspaper reports of illegal abortions in New York and elsewhere spread around the country, opposition to abortion grew among the American populace.

The result of this "Great Awakening" about the tragedy of abortion was the passage of statutes between 1860 and 1890 which greatly strengthened legal restrictions on abortions, especially in the early months of gestation before "quickening."[38] Riddle also explains that the anti-abortion movement in the nineteenth century was the result of a greater understanding about the development of human life within the womb. When the *American Medical Association* began its campaign in 1857 to

29. Brodie, 154.
30. Cited in Mohr, 193.
31. Ibid., 193.
32. Cited in ibid., 186.
33. Jacoby, 62.
34. Mohr, 181.
35. Ibid., 178.
36. Ibid., 179.
37. Ibid., 179.
38. Brodie, 254.

eradicate abortion, it was also working to educate the public against the commonly held, but now refuted, view that an unborn child is only "alive" after quickening.[39]

> " . . . this child is a man for whose life the Son of God has died, for whose unavoidable part in the guilt of all humanity, and future individual guilt he has already paid the price. The true light of the world shines already in the darkness of the mother's womb."
>
> –Karl Barth

This new understanding of the continuous development of the unborn child most likely precipitated changes in Roman Catholic canon law as well, which had until that time recognized a distinction between the abortion of "formed" and "unformed" fetuses. In 1869, Pope Pius IX renewed the church law against the practice of abortion, applying an automatic excommunication against anyone who was involved in the procurement of an abortion, and he also removed any differences between penances for early and late-term abortions.[40]

It is also noteworthy that until the 1950s there was a virtual unanimity of opinion among Christian theologians on the abortion question. For instance, Karl Barth, probably the best known theologian of the twentieth century and the founder of neo-orthodoxy wrote, "Our first contention must be that no pretext can alter the fact that the whole circle of those concerned is in the strict sense engaged in the killing of human life. For the unborn child is from the very first a child. It is still developing and has no independent life. But it is a man and not a thing, not a mere part of the mother's body."[41] He added,

> . . . we must underline the fact that he who destroys germinating life kills a man and thus ventures the monstrous thing of decreeing concerning the life and death of a fellow-man whose life is given by God and therefore, like his own, belongs to Him. He desires to discharge a divine office, or, even if not, he accepts responsibility for such a discharge, by daring to have the last word on at least the temporal form of the life of his fellow man. . . . Moreover, this child is a man for whose life the Son of God has died, for

39. Riddle, *Eve's Herbs*, 222.

40. Ibid., 223.

41. Karl Barth, *Church Dogmatics*, vol. 4, part 4. (Edinburgh: T & T Clark, 1961), 415.

whose unavoidable part in the guilt of all humanity, and future individual guilt he has already paid the price. The true light of the world shines already in the darkness of the mother's womb.[42]

Dietrich Bonhoeffer, the brilliant Lutheran theologian and pastor who was executed by the Nazis during World War II, wrote this about abortion,

> Marriage involves acknowledgement of the right of life that is to come into being, a right which is not subject to the disposal of the married couple. Unless this right is acknowledged as a matter of principle, marriage ceases to be marriage and becomes a mere liaison ... Destruction of the embryo in the mother's womb is a violation of the right to live which God has bestowed upon this nascent life. To raise the question whether we are here concerned already with a human being or not is merely to confuse the issue. The simple fact is that God certainly intended to create a human being and that this nascent human being has been deliberately deprived of his life. And that is nothing but murder. A great many different motives may lead to an action of this kind; indeed in cases where it is an act of despair, performed in circumstances of extreme human or economic destitution and misery, the guilt may often lie rather with the community than with the individual. Precisely in this connexion, money may conceal many a wanton deed, while the poor man's more reluctant lapse may far more easily be disclosed. All these considerations must no doubt have quite a decisive influence on our personal and pastoral attitude towards the person concerned, but they cannot in any way alter the fact of murder.[43]

In addition, Jürgen Moltmann, the famous Reformed theologian whose groundbreaking 1972 book, *The Crucified God*, reopened discussions on God the Father's impassibility (the belief that God the Father is unable to suffer), had this to say about abortion,

> Every devaluation of the fetus, the embryo, and the fertilized ovum compared with life that is already born and adult is the beginning of a rejection and a de-humanization of human beings. Hope for the resurrection of the body does not permit any such death sentence to be passed on life. Fundamentally speaking, human beings mutilate themselves when embryos are devalued into mere

---

42. Barth, 416.

43. Dietrich Bonhoeffer, *Ethics.* (New York: Touchstone, 1955), 173–74.

"human material," for every human being was once just such an embryo in need of protection.[44]

In short, the attitudes of theologians from the Reformation until the 1960s show an almost unanimous opinion for protecting human life from the moment of conception. From the Great Reformation thinkers Luther and Calvin, to the writings of prominent theologians in the early twentieth century such as Barth, Bonhoeffer, and Moltmann, the Christian witness has been consistently pro-life. Nor can a forerunner in the Protestant faith be found for the pro-choice Christians of today.

Now that the irrefutable pro-life witness of the church has been demonstrated, chapter 6 will look at the most outspoken pro-choice Christians, the *Religious Coalition for Reproductive Choice* and their allies, to see if their pro-choice testimonies pass the "reality check" of the biblical witness and the history of the Christian faith.

44. Cited in Michael J. Gorman and Ann Loar Brooks, *Holy Abortion?* 58.

6

Breaking from Tradition

The Religious Coalition for Reproductive Choice and Other Pro-Choice Christian Groups

CHRISTIANS WHO HAVE TAKEN the position that abortion should be readily available and in no way regulated have received a great deal of media coverage since the 1960s. Many articles have been written on the abortion statements of individual Christian denominations, and on the vociferous debates that have occurred at many of their denominational conventions. Christian pro-choice organizations have often been cited in these stories, with groups like *Catholics for a Free Choice* and the *Religious Coalition for Reproductive Choice* (*RCRC*) depicted as prominent Christian voices in favor of abortion.

Many pro-choice Christian authors and theologians have also attempted to provide an intellectual foundation for their views. For instance, the Roman Catholic Marquette University professor Daniel C. Maguire (who was recently censured by the *United States Conference of Catholic Bishops*) attempted to show that abortion was morally acceptable in his book, *Sacred Choices: The Right to Contraception and Abortion in Ten World Religions*. In *Sacred Choices*, Maguire proposes that the pro-life position was only one of a number of acceptable positions on abortion over the history of the Catholic Church,[1] a theory that has already been

---

1. Anne Hendershott, *The Politics of Abortion*. (New York: Encounter Books, 2006), 91.

refuted. He also states that "these [pro-choice] traditions are richer, more sensitive, and more subtle than we might believe."[2]

But Maguire spends very little time explaining the history of these alleged traditions, nor does he discuss the development of a child in the womb or whether he or she has a right to be born. Largely ignoring these important issues, Maguire instead chooses to fill his work with long sections that deprecate pro-lifers and pro-life denominations.

For instance, Maguire discusses the pro-life alliance in the United Nations between the Vatican and Muslim Countries on votes concerning abortion. He alleges that this alliance is not motivated by a mutual desire among Catholics and Muslims to defend children in the womb, but instead implies that their main motivation is sexism.[3] In *Sacred Choices* he writes, "[are] these two patriarchical bastions . . . bonded in the face of a new threat—the emergence of free, self determining women?"[4]

Maguire makes numerous other dubious claims, including the assertion that the Catholic Church's position against abortion is unofficial[5] even though it has been consistently proclaimed by countless popes and councils throughout history. He also asserts that its pro-life position is motivated by a preference for the celibate lifestyle.[6]

But this outdated belief that the Catholic Church has a "hang-up" about sex simply does not correspond with contemporary Catholic teaching on the subject. The following November 21, 1979 quote by Pope John Paul II amply demonstrates that the Catholic tradition recognizes the value of sexual pleasure within marriage while it emphasizes sex's unitive and self-giving aspects. He writes,

> Uniting with each other (in the conjugal act) so closely as to become "one flesh" . . . is a powerful bond established by the Creator. Through it they discover their own humanity, both in its original unity, and in the duality of a mysterious mutual attraction. However, sex is something more than the mysterious power of human corporality, which acts almost by virtue of instinct. At the level of man and in the mutual relationship of persons, sex expresses an ever

2. Daniel C. Maguire, *Sacred Choices: the Right to Contraception and Abortion in Ten World Religions.* (Minneapolis, MN: Fortress Press, 2001), vii.

3. Ibid., 39.

4. Ibid., 31.

5. Ibid., 35.

6. Ibid., 34.

new surpassing of the limit of man's solitude that is inherent in the constitution of his body, and determines its original meaning. This surpassing always contains within it a certain assumption of the solicitude of the body of the second "self" as one's own.[7]

In *Sacred Choices*, Maguire paints fundamentalist Christians with the same brush as he does Catholics, stating that their stand on abortion is a "reaction to the emergence of free women and the loss of male monopoly."[8] To add insult to injury, he characterizes the desire to prohibit abortion as a "fascistic impulse."[9] Maguire even likens the unity between pro-life Catholics and fundamentalists to Herod and Pontius Pilate's cooperation in crucifying Jesus in Luke 23:12.[10]

Another outspoken pro-choice Christian writer is the United Church of Christ minister Tom Davis. In his book *Sacred Work*, Davis attempts to make the case that abortion, and specifically *Planned Parenthood's* involvement in the abortion business, is a "sacred work."[11] One might realistically ask how this could be the case. If we refer back to the biblical witness, we find just the opposite, since Jewish and Christian communities in the Bible were actively working against the pagan practices of abortion, infanticide, and exposure. So how can a truly Christian case be made for defending abortion? As has been previously seen in Maguire's work, one must either obscure the facts or bypass the central issues altogether.

In *Sacred Work*, Davis takes this second tack. Just as was seen in Maguire's *Sacred Choices*, the ethical problem of killing an unborn child in the womb is hardly discussed, and instead Davis concentrates on the mother and how denying her the right to destroy her child in utero somehow violates the biblical principle of assisting widows and orphans. Davis quotes Exodus 22:22, "You shall not abuse any widow or orphan,"[12] and he implies that any effort to limit abortion is an abuse of a disenfranchised group, i.e. women. But there is absolutely no indication that Davis' interpretation is within the biblical author's intent.

---

7. John Paul II, *The Theology of the Body: Human Love in the Divine Plan.* (Boston. MA: Pauline Books and Media, 1997), 49–50.

8. Maguire, 123.

9. Ibid., 129.

10. Ibid., 127.

11. Tom Davis, *Sacred Work.* (New Brunswick, NJ: Rutgers University Press, 2005), 6.

12. Ibid., 6.

Probably one of the best-researched works from the pro-choice side in recent years is the aforementioned *Brief, Liberal, Catholic Defense of Abortion* written by Daniel Dombrowski and Robert Deltete, two philosophy professors from the University of Seattle. In the book, Dombrowski and Deltete attempt to promote the pro-choice view by restructuring the church's opposition to abortion into what they called the "ontological" and "perversity" reasons.[13] According to the authors, the church's "ontological" reason for the sinfulness of abortion is its belief that a fetus is a human being (and therefore has a right to life). And the "perversity" reason is the church's theology that abortion is sinful because it is a perversion of sexual relations.[14]

In discussing the "ontological" reason, the authors use an argument that has been heard and refuted before: Augustine and Aquinas did not believe that the abortion of an early or "unformed" fetus should be punished as murder, and therefore early abortions should not be seen as sinful.[15] In reviewing the "perversity" reason, Dombrowski and Deltete discuss Augustine's belief that sexual relations should only be undertaken for the purposes of procreation.[16] They then propose that Augustine opposed early abortion solely for the reason that it adulterated the sanctity of sex by ending its procreative function.[17]

Their conclusion is that since Augustine and Aquinas (under the "ontological" reason) did not consider an early-term abortion to be the equivalent of murder, and since Augustine's "perversity" reason is based on the outdated sexual "hang-up" that intercourse is only valuable for procreation, early-term abortions *should* be permissible.

But there are a number of flaws to this theory. The first is that Augustine and Aquinas are merely two, albeit important, theologians in the history of the church. As we have already reviewed and the authors themselves admit,[18] some of the church fathers such as Tertullian and Basil's brother, Gregory, the Bishop of Nyssa, viewed abortion as murder from the moment of conception. There is also little evidence that Augustine

---

13. Dombrowski and Deltete, 2–3.

14. Ibid., 2–3.

15. Ibid., 2–3.

16. Ibid., 2–3.

17. Ibid., 2–3.

18. Ibid., 27–28.

and Aquinas believed that a young fetus lacked "ontological" value (even if an early abortion might not have been legally considered murder). The quote I provided earlier strongly suggests that Augustine did recognize an "ontological" right to life for the early-term unborn child. Furthermore, Augustine's and Aquinas' views would have been deeply influenced by the Greek translation of Exodus 21:22–25, which, as has been noted before, recognized that the killing of an early-term unborn child was a punishable crime—that is, it was sinful on "ontological" grounds alone, without any reference to "perversity" reasons.

One must also question Dombrowski and Deltete's willingness to throw out the "perversity" reason for the sinfulness of abortion on the grounds that it is outdated. Today's Christian might justifiably reject Augustine's belief that sex should only be engaged in for procreative purposes. However, that same person would undoubtedly agree with the kernel of the "perversity" argument, which is that abortion is highly destructive to the marital relationship and should therefore be rejected. Indeed, how could anyone, even in today's society, deny that abortion adulterates the true spirit of marriage?

Dombrowski and Deltete also show no consistency when they recognize a child to be "formed" or "unformed." While they cite Augustine's and Aquinas' theories of formation (traditionally interpreted by canon law to be at forty days), they use their own estimation of true humanity to be at the point of "sentiency"—the full development of a central nervous system (between 24 and 32 weeks).[19] While this point of "sentiency" is theologically baseless, its dating seems to fit nicely with the authors' original view of the acceptability of abortion during the first two trimesters, and the immorality of third-trimester abortions. But later in the book, Dombrowski and Deltete contradict themselves, and allow even these very late-term abortions in the cases of a danger to a mother's health (not necessarily a life-threatening danger) or a "life diminishing" deformity in the child.[20]

The authors also reveal their motives when they admit that they see nothing sinful in pre-marital sex,[21] homosexual sex,[22] or in viewing

19. Dombrowski and Deltete, 56.
20. Ibid., 127.
21. Ibid., 86.
22. Ibid., 86.

pornography,[23] unless these acts result in a lack of "agapic mutual respect"[24] for one's "partner." These admissions seem to indicate that *A Brief, Liberal, Catholic Defense of Abortion* is simply part of an overall strategy to remove traditional morality from the faith. As such, this well-researched book appears to be a vehicle for advancing the authors' own agendas rather than an unbiased search for God's will on the abortion issue.

Organized pro-choice Christian groups have, over the years, provided an activist network for the abortion apologists discussed above. One group, called *Catholics for a Free Choice*, was directed for nearly three decades by Frances Kissling, a former novitiate of the Sisters of Saint Joseph, and also a former director of an abortion clinic.[25] Kissling, who retired in 2007, believes that the Bible is silent on the morality of abortion, and that no one really knows when a fetus becomes a human being.[26] In saying this, she has attempted to justify abortion by pointing to the diversity of opinion among theologians regarding fetal development. As discussed before, there has been some debate over the history of the Christian church about when a child is "formed" or "ensouled." But surprisingly, the question of when a fetus becomes a human being is of little value in deciding whether abortion is ethical or not. This is because Christian theologians on both sides of these debates have almost always agreed that abortion is sinful from the moment of conception, regardless of whether the fetus is "formed" or "ensouled."

Catholics for a Free Choice has been funded by numerous liberal charitable organizations, including the *Ford Foundation* and Hugh Hefner's *Playboy Foundation*.[27] The organization has also insulted numerous Catholics by printing prayer cards with the image of Our Lady of Guadalupe (the patron saint of unborn children) on them, and the words "Keep Abortion Legal" on the back.[28]

The *Religious Coalition for Reproductive Choice (RCRC)* has also been very active in promoting its pro-choice perspective within the church. Led by the Rev. Carlton W. Veazey, a *National Baptist Convention USA*

23. Dombrowski and Deltete, 85–86.

24. Ibid., 87.

25. Hendershott, 98.

26. Ibid., 98.

27. Ibid., 98.

28. Ibid., 100.

minister,[29] *RCRC* operates out of twenty-two affiliate chapters across the country,[30] and has even created a seminary curriculum called "Theology and Reproductive Choice," which is used to teach the morality of abortion in many seminaries across the United States.[31] *RCRC* has also been active in grass-roots activism, even calling upon the clergy to personally "bless" abortion clinics.[32] The major Christian denominations which were early members of *RCRC* included the *American Baptist Church*, the *Episcopal Church*, the two denominations which became the *Presbyterian Church (USA)*, the *United Church of Christ*, the *United Methodist Church*, and the *Christian Church (Disciples of Christ)*.[33]

Originally called the *Religious Coalition for Abortion Rights* when the organization was created in 1973,[34] it changed its name to its current *Religious Coalition for Reproductive Choice* in 1994,[35] probably out of a desire to remove the word "abortion," a word that today is often negatively received, from its title.

Like the pro-choice theologians quoted above, *RCRC* theologians utilize a radical and highly unorthodox interpretation of the Bible to legitimize and advocate for abortion-on-demand. Katherine Hancock Ragsdale, an Episcopal priest and former chairman of the board of *RCRC*, compares pro-choice Christian activists to those whom Jesus preached the beatitudes by paraphrasing Matthew 5:11–12, "Blessed are you [pro-choice Christian activists] when people revile you and persecute you falsely on my account, for in the same way they persecuted the prophets who were before you."[36] The comparison between those who actively

29. "Coalition President" in Religious Coalition for Reproductive Choice website. (Washington, D.C. July 2006 [cited 24 August 2007]); available from http://www.rcrc.org/about/president.cfm; INTERNET.

30. Gorman and Brooks, 4.

31. Hendershott, 91.

32. Ibid., 90.

33. Gorman and Brooks, 6.

34. Solinger, Rickie, ed. *Abortion Wars: A Half Century of Struggle 1950–2000*. (Berkeley: University of California Press, 1998), xiii.

35. Loretta J. Ross, "African American Women," in *Abortion Wars: A Half Century of Struggle 1950–2000*, ed. by Rickie Solinger (Berkeley: University of California Press, 1998), 199.

36. Katherine Hancock Ragsdale, "Faithful Witness for Choice," in *Prayerfully Pro-Choice: Resources for Worship*. (Washington, D.C.: Religious Coalition for Reproductive Choice, 2000), 31.

advocate the killing of unborn life and those who shared the gospel of life is clearly unwarranted.

Another adulteration of the biblical message has come from ethicist and *RCRC* contributor Dr. Paul Simmons. Simmons wrote a commentary on Genesis 1 and 3, which seemingly gave every woman the power of creation over human life, an attribute that can only be possessed by God. He writes, "Because the pregnancy is hers, the decision to continue the pregnancy is uniquely hers. Like the Creator, she reflects upon what is good for the creation of which she is agent."[37]

This tendency of *RCRC* to delegate divine authority to women[38] can also be seen in the *RCRC* decision-making liturgy called "You Are Not Alone: Seeking Wisdom to Decide." This liturgy, which was written by Diann Neu, who is the codirector of the *Women's Alliance for Theology, Ethics, and Ritual (WATER)*,[39] speaks of a deified "Wisdom" who lives within in every woman. This "Wisdom" works to guide each woman in making holy decisions. She writes, "Wisdom lives within us. Listen to her. Trust her. Talk with her whenever you need to. She is your friend. She is the Holy One who is with you always. Seek to find wisdom and love her fiercely."[40] The liturgy concludes with a song which explains that God is found in one-self.[41] The only conclusion that can be drawn from this liturgy is that the truth does not come from God and his Holy Word, but rather from within each person.

> "You are to claim your godlike, God-given role in creation by saying yes or no, secure in the knowledge that whatever you decide, after having honestly sought what is right, God will bless . . ."
>
> —George F. Luthringer

---

37. Paul D. Simmons, "Some Biblical References to Personhood," in *Prayerfully Pro-Choice: Resources for Worship.* (Washington, D.C.: Religious Coalition for Reproductive Choice, 2000), 117.

38. Gorman and Brooks, 17.

39. Diane Neu, "Affirming a Choice," in *Prayerfully Pro-Choice: Resources for Worship.* (Washington, D.C.: Religious Coalition for Reproductive Choice, 2000), 82.

40. Diann Neu, "You Are Not Alone: Seeking Wisdom to Decide," in *Prayerfully Pro-Choice: Resources for Worship.* (Washington, D.C.: Religious Coalition for Reproductive Choice, 2000), 81.

41. Ibid., 81.

This type of *RCRC* self-deification (and the assurance of God's blessing regardless of the choice one arrives at)[42] can also be seen in George F. Luthringer's *Considering Abortion? Clarifying What You Believe*. Luthringer, an assisting priest at St. Columba's Episcopal Church in Camarillo, CA writes, "You are to claim your godlike, God-given role in creation by saying yes or no, secure in the knowledge that whatever you decide, after having honestly sought what is right, God will bless. . . "[43] But what is not explained in the work is why God would bless a violation of His holy law, regardless of how "honestly [it was] sought."[44]

Even more dubious theology can be found in *RCRC*'s "Ceremony for Closure after an Abortion." In that liturgy, Unitarian Universalist minister Rev. Dr. Kendyl Gibbons writes, "Not every essence shall come to be; / It is in choosing that we are free."[45] But is this cavalier attitude about human life helpful to the post-abortive woman? The average person might justifiably come to the conclusion that the "essences" do not come to be because someone has ended their lives. So this liturgy seems to be skirting the question of *why* every "essence" does not come to be. In addition, one might biblically conclude that it is in Jesus Christ that we are free (Romans 8:2), and that unfettered choice is in no way the source of our freedom, as this ceremony suggests.

In this liturgy, Gibbons also veers off into a theological worldview that is reminiscent of gnosticism with its *aeons* of deities emanating from and then returning to a central godhead. She writes, "with loving grief, we release that potential to other incarnations in the infinite womb of the universe, from which nothing is ever lost."[46] In other words, to assuage the guilt of a woman who has experienced abortion, one must resort to heretical theologies which were discredited nearly two millennia ago.

In another *RCRC* document called "Word of Hope," Rev. Dr. James Armstrong, a United Church of Christ minister writes, "A woman's body belongs to that woman . . . a woman has the right to make that choice

---

42. Gorman and Brooks, 29.

43. George Luthringer, *Considering Abortion? Clarifying What You Believe*. (Washington, D.C.: Religious Coalition for Reproductive Choice, 1992), 6.

44. Ibid., 6.

45. Kendyl Gibbons, "Ceremony for Closure after an Abortion," in *Prayerfully Pro-Choice: Resources for Worship*. (Washington, D.C.: Religious Coalition for Reproductive Choice, 2000), 86.

46. Ibid., 86.

[abortion] within the sacred precincts of her own soul."[47] Michael Gorman and Ann Loar Brooks, in their book *Holy Abortion?* contrast this statement with 1 Corinthians 6:19–20, "Do you not know that your body is a temple of the Holy Spirit, who is in you, whom you have received from God? *You are not your own*; you were bought at a price. Therefore honor God with your body. [italics added]"[48] Indeed, the Bible clears up Armstrong's misconception—our bodies are not our own, but are rather the possessions of God.

Gorman and Brooks have also pointed out that *RCRC* has, in its resources, often portrayed a "hands off" God who has allowed women the complete freedom to make any moral decision with regard to childbirth or abortion. Instead of the biblical vision of a chosen people who are totally dependent on God for moral guidance, the *RCRC* "god" has stayed out of the ethical arena and has left all such decisions up to mankind.[49]

Probably the most disturbing *RCRC* liturgy is called "Affirming a Choice," written by Diann Neu. In it she writes that, "This liturgy affirms that a woman has made a good and holy decision to have an abortion."[50] The liturgy also includes a "Prayer to Mother Goddess and Father God" that praises these deities for giving women and men "the power of choice."[51] Besides the fact that "Affirming a Choice" ignores the two thousand year history of Christian doctrine on abortion, its most egregious error is that it attempts to justify the sin of abortion through communal worship. One can only imagine that such a liturgy will only harden burdened hearts to the sins they have committed, rather than cleanse those hearts through the grace of forgiveness.

The *Religious Coalition for Reproductive Choice* has also used the so-called world "population explosion" to call for the worldwide availability of abortion. In 1999, the year when the world's population reached six billion people, Marjorie Signer of *RCRC* and Cynthia Cooper of the *Center for Reproductive Law and Policy* delivered a speech that advocated an increase in international abortion services. In that speech, entitled "Six Billion People—A Matter of Consequence," they stressed that "affordable

47. James Armstrong, "Word of Hope," in *Prayerfully Pro-Choice: Resources for Worship.* (Washington, D.C.: Religious Coalition for Reproductive Choice, 2000), 38.

48. Gorman and Brooks, 28.

49. Ibid., 28.

50. Ibid., 82.

51. Ibid., 82.

abortion services" were vital for achieving the eschatological vision described in Isaiah 65:20–23, which prophesized that the chosen people
would one day be freed from "bear[ing] children in calamity."[52] When one
steps back and looks at this assertion, one can only reach the conclusion
that Signer and Cooper must believe that God's plan for a perfect world
includes the funding of millions of international abortions.

This chapter has revealed the often misleading biblical exegesis
employed by *RCRC*, *Catholics for a Free Choice*, and other pro-choice
Christians on the abortion question. Their views have also been demonstrated to be inconsistent with the traditions of the Christian church. One
can only conclude that these adherents of pro-choice Christianity have
created new and unfounded biblical interpretations in order to create a
theology of abortion which, quite simply, does not exist.

The next chapter will take a look at Christian denominational his-
tories since the 1960s in regard to abortion. Many denominations during
these years have maintained a strong defense of the sanctity of human life.
Even in those churches which strayed from traditional teaching on the
sinfulness of abortion, there have been many courageous Christians who
have testified to their denominations' errors, and have boldly defended
human life in the womb.

---

52. Marjorie Signer and Cynthia Cooper, "Six Billion People—a Matter of Consequence," in *Prayerfully Pro-Choice: Resources for Worship*. (Washington, D.C.: Religious
Coalition for Reproductive Choice, 2000), 99.

7

Controversy

Denominational Activity on the Abortion Question Since the 1960s

A S LATE AS 1961, the *National Council of Churches*, an organization which includes most of the American mainline Protestant denominations, issued a resolution which condemned the practice of abortion unless it was required to save the life or health of the mother.[1] But in the following year, the abortion reform movement began to emerge among many Christian mainline denominations, with the *United Presbyterian Church*, now part of the *Presbyterian Church USA*, calling for the reform of abortion laws, and the *American Lutheran Church*, now part of the *Evangelical Lutheran Church of America (ELCA)*, making a similar shift in teaching in 1963.[2] In 1967, twenty-one Protestant ministers and rabbis started the *Clergy Consultation Service*, which was led by the Rev. Howard Moody, an American Baptist minister from New York.[3] This organization was created to provide a referral service for women seeking illegal abortions. It soon added Chicago-based operations in 1969,[4] and grew quickly,

1. Randall E. Otto, "The Relativism of Pro-Choice Ethics," in *Affirming Life: Biblical Perspectives on Abortion for the United Church of Christ,* ed. by John B. Brown Jr. and Robin Fox (Princeton, NJ: Princeton University Press, 1991), 2.

2. J. Christopher Soper, *Evangelical Christianity in the United States and Great Britain.* (New York: New York University Press, 1994), 146.

3. James Risen and Judy Thomas, *Wrath of Angels: The American Abortion War.* (New York: Basic Books, 1998), 20.

4. Loretta J. Ross, "African American Women," in *Abortion Wars: A Half Century of Struggle 1950–2000,* ed. by Rickie Solinger, Berkeley: University of California Press, 1998), 178.

becoming active in twenty states before *Roe v. Wade,* the U.S. Supreme Court decision which legalized abortion in all fifty states in 1973.[5]

In those pre-*Roe* years, the *Clergy Consultation Service* referred women to abortion service providers as far away as Puerto Rico, Mexico City, and England.[6] The creation of the *Clergy Consultation Service* also marked the beginning of active, organized clergy involvement in the pro-choice movement.

In spite of some Christian denominations' pro-choice positions, many clergymen and women also came to the defense of preborn human life. What follows is a review of the pro-life activity that has occurred since the 1960s in the major Christian traditions in the United States. Chapter 8 will attempt to provide a more quantitative analysis of the percentage of right-to-life adherents within worldwide Christianity.

AFRICAN AMERICAN DENOMINATIONS

In 1977, the oldest African American Christian denomination, the *African Methodist Episcopal Church (AMEC),* published a study called, "Consideration of the Abortion Issue," in which it took a strong pro-life stand (see Appendix I). This statement seems to be the denomination's latest official word on the matter, since no more recent documentation was received from a request from the denomination's historiographer. The largest African American denomination, the *National Baptist Convention, USA,* does not have a denominational statement on abortion since its congregations are autonomous, and teaching on ethical issues, like abortion, is left up to its individual congregations. It is also noteworthy that neither denomination directly speaks to the issue of abortion on its website, a practice which is common among U.S. Christian denominations.

Pro-life African American clergy have explained that this silence concerning the sanctity of life does not indicate a pro-choice position by these churches. Rather, it shows that abortion is commonly dismissed as a moral issue worthy of much attention,[7] and is often overshadowed by other ethical concerns such as racism, education, drugs, and gangs.[8] This indifference may also be due to a general lack of information about the

---

5. Soper, 107.

6. Ross, 178.

7. Joseph Parker, telephone interview by author, August 27, 2007.

8. Luke J. Robinson, interview with the author, December 20, 2007, Frederick, MD.

high rate of abortions that occur within the black community.[9] However, it would be wrong to assume that there are no actively pro-choice clergy with these denominations. For instance, the president of *RCRC*, Carlton Veazey, is a *National Baptist Convention, USA* pastor.

Despite the low priority that has been given to the issue of abortion by most African American churches, many black church leaders have taken the lead to defend Christianity's traditional stand on the sanctity of human life. Probably the most influential pro-life activist within the African American community today is the Rev. Johnny Hunter, who currently serves at the Cliffdale Community Church in Fayetteville, North Carolina, and is the National Director of the black pro-life organization *Life Education and Resource Network (LEARN)*.[10] In referencing abortion's role in eliminating the next generation of blacks, Rev. Hunter has bluntly stated that "abortionists have eliminated more African American children than the KKK ever lynched."[11]

During his pro-life ministry, Hunter has convinced many women not to abort. One of those times came after preaching a sermon at New Covenant Church in Buffalo, New York. His message to the congregation, including those contemplating abortion, was "Who knows what my child will become?"[12] A young woman who was in the congregation that day could not stop those words from repeating in her mind. She later told Rev. Hunter that she had gone to an abortion clinic later that week and had even paid the $300 fee for the procedure, but while waiting to see the doctor she changed her mind and decided to have her baby. Hunter had the privilege of later baptizing the mother and dedicating her child to the Lord.[13]

Hunter organized *LEARN* at a meeting in Houston, Texas in 1993, in an attempt to better organize the nation's disparate African-American pro-life advocates. The organization was also started to provide educational resources on the sanctity of life to black Americans. Over the years, *LEARN* has also been blessed with a number of very dedicated activists. For instance, its Chairman of the Board is the physician and former

9. Robinson.

10. Johnny Hunter, telephone interview with the author, December 27, 2007.

11. Hendershott, 33.

12. Hunter.

13. Ibid.

abortion provider Dr. Haywood Robinson, who stopped performing the procedure after he experienced a conversion at a concert by Christian singer Leon Patillo. Today, Robinson responds to the "safe sex" message by teaching that there is no such thing as "safe sin."[14] He is joined by fellow physician and *LEARN* member Dr. John Biggs, who has made the abstinence message a priority within that organization.[15]

One of the strongest pro-life voices in the AME Church has been Pastor Luke J. Robinson of Quinn Chapel AME Church in Frederick, Maryland.[16] Pastor Robinson took up the pro-life ministry in the early 1980s by participating in local pro-life demonstrations and by preaching the gospel of life on Christian radio.[17] Since that time, he has worked with *LEARN* to publicize the high incidence of abortion within the African-American community.[18] As the keynote speaker at the January 22, 2007 *March for Life* in Washington, D.C., Pastor Robinson explained that although blacks were only 12% of the U.S. population, 34% of all U.S. abortions were performed on African-American women.[19] He also decried the fact that the nation's black leadership ignored the issue and considered it unimportant. He said, "Abortion is not a non-issue—it is a major issue in our community. Nothing has killed more blacks than abortion. Of the 17 million blacks killed [by abortion] since 1973, how many Martin Luther Kings have been destroyed?"[20] Pastor Robinson has also presented the black pro-life message at *National Right to Life* and *Care Net* conferences, as well as at *AMEC* conventions.[21] He has also been named a consultant to the *AMEC* Social Action Committee, in recognition of his efforts to raise awareness about the sinfulness of abortion within that denomination.[22]

Also noteworthy has been black pro-life leader and street activist Rev. Clenard Childress, Senior Pastor of New Calvary Baptist Church in Montclair, New Jersey, and the president of the Northeast Region of *LEARN*. Childress has pointed out that the silence of black Christians on

14. Hunter.
15. Ibid.
16. Ibid.
17. Robinson.
18. Ibid.
19. Ibid.
20. Ibid.
21. Ibid.
22. Parker.

the abortion issue is due to their traditional allegiance to the Democratic Party rather than indicative of an overwhelming pro-choice attitude among blacks.[23] His powerful website, www.blackgenocide.org, shows how *Planned Parenthood*, the nation's largest abortion provider, targets minorities, and how 78% of its abortion clinics reside in minority neighborhoods.[24] Rev. Childress, like many African American activists, has spoken against *Planned Parenthood* because of that organization's early efforts to use birth control to limit the growth of the black population. This eugenic effort called the "Negro Project" was begun in 1938, and it targeted poor blacks in the South.[25] Childress has also been active in numerous street demonstrations, such as the *Walk for Life West Coast*, to bring awareness to the abortion problem.

Martin Luther King's niece, Dr. Alveda C. King, has also been a prominent speaker within the pro-life movement. An accomplished author, academic, and former Georgia state legislator, King sees the abortion question in terms of a struggle for civil rights.[26] During the marches for black equality in the 1960s, King's home in Birmingham, Alabama was bombed in an effort to silence her uncle's message.[27] She uses these powerful experiences to once again speak out in favor of civil rights, but today, she fights for the rights of children yet unborn. In her appearances, King explains how our nation's current policy of abortion-on-demand, with its disproportionate effect on the African-American population, is inconsistent with Martin Luther King's "dream." As an ordained minister and a post-abortive woman, she also powerfully shares her own experiences with abortion and the forgiveness of Jesus Christ.

Another outspoken pro-life African-American woman is Day Gardner, who is the Media Director of the *National Pro-Life Action Center*, and a news anchor for *National Pro-Life Radio*.[28] A former Miss

23. Hendershott, 33.

24. Ibid., 33.

25. Angela Franks, *Margaret Sanger's Eugenic Legacy: The Control of Female Fertility.* (Jefferson, NC: McFarland and Co., 2005), 44.

26. Alveda C. King, "Dr. Alveda C. King," from the King for America website. (Atlanta, GA [cited 18 December 2007]) available from http://www.kingforamerica.com/adkfoundation_article2.htm.

27. Ibid.

28. "Day Gardner," from the National Pro-Life Action Center web page. (Washington, D.C. [cited 27 December 2007]) available from http://www.nplac.org/bios/bio-dgardner .html; INTERNET.

Delaware, Ms. Gardner was the first black woman to make it to the semi-final round of the Miss America pageant.[29] In 2002, during an unsuccessful campaign for a seat in the Maryland State Legislature, Gardner learned that the African-American abortion rate was much higher than the national average.[30] Like many other black pro-life activists, this data convinced her of the urgent need to educate the African-American community about the abortion epidemic.

In 2003, Ms. Gardner became president of *Black Americans for Life*, an outreach organization of the *National Right to Life Committee*.[31] In 2006, she joined the *National Pro-Life Action Center*, and also started her own African American pro-life organization, the *National Black Pro-Life Union*.[32] A lifelong Christian, Gardner values the need to preach the gospel of life within African-American churches. But she also recognizes the limitations of this strategy, since the black church is no longer the "town hall" that it once was in the 1950s and 1960s.[33] This realization has motivated her to create media messages which resonate with both Christian and non-Christian black women in crisis pregnancies.[34]

Rev. Joseph Parker, the pastor of Campbell Chapel AME Church in Pulaski, Tennessee, has also been a highly visible pro-life black leader. An outspoken preacher on the right to life, Reverend Parker has also written a dramatic play called "Rev. Riding in the Hood," which has been performed in a number of AME churches in the South.[35] The play depicts the fictional character Mr. Brown, who finds that his unwed daughter has become pregnant.[36] In attempting to decide whether to urge his daughter to keep the child or to have an abortion, Mr. Brown discusses the matter with his pastor, Reverend Riding, who educates him on the abortion issue.[37] Through his growing understanding of God's plan for human life, Mr. Brown guides the audience to the pro-life position.[38]

29. "Day Gardner."

30. Day Gardner. E-mail interview with the author, December 23, 2007.

31. Ibid.

32. Ibid.

33. Ibid.

34. Ibid.

35. Parker.

36. Ibid.

37. Ibid.

38. Ibid.

BAPTISTS

The American Baptist Convention became one of the first Christian denominations to enter the pro-choice movement when it voted to support the reform of abortion laws in May of 1967.[39] Originally a member of the *Religious Coalition for Reproductive Choice*, the American Baptist position became more moderate during the 1970s and 1980s. In 1986, it ended its relationship with the more radical *RCRC*.[40]

Yet the moderate pro-choice view held by the American Baptist denomination belies an overall pro-life position by most Baptist churches in the United States. One of the most prominent pro-life Baptists in the 1970s was the Rev. Billy Graham, who encouraged the creation of the *Christian Action Council*, which was founded by Harold O.J. Brown and C. Everett Koop in 1975. This organization, now called *Care Net*, is an umbrella group for Crisis Pregnancy Centers (CPCs) across the United States.[41] *Care Net*'s hundreds of centers have worked diligently to assist women in crisis pregnancies, providing them with pregnancy tests, counseling and medical services, and financial assistance. Through its selfless efforts, *Care Net* has saved countless women and their unborn children from the trauma of abortion.

Another outspoken Baptist was the late Rev. Jerry Falwell, who defended the sanctity of life on his *Old Time Gospel Hour* television show. The staff of the television show also wrote the powerful book, *Judgment without Justice: The Dred Scott and Roe v. Wade Decisions*, which compared the pro-choice and pro-slavery movements. *Judgment without Justice* convincingly draws parallels between the famous Supreme Court decisions, and it shows how *Dred Scott* and *Roe v. Wade*, in a similar ways, characterized both African Americans and the unborn as sub-human.[42]

Always steadfast, Falwell was often out in front of the abortion debate, and he characterized abortion as "America's national sin."[43] He also worked within the political arena to change the American policy of abortion-on-demand through his political lobbying organization *Moral*

---

39. Risen and Thomas, 14.

40. Gorman and Brooks, 43.

41. Risen and Thomas, 152.

42. Jacoby, 84.

43. Cynthia Gorney, *Articles of Faith: A Frontline History of the Abortion Wars.* (New York: Simon and Schuster, 1998), 346.

Majority, which he started in 1979.[44] This organization, soon after its creation, boasted that it was in touch with 72,000 preachers, educating them on how to influence pro-life candidates and legislation.[45] In its heyday during the early 1980s, the *Moral Majority* boasted around 2 million members.[46]

Falwell's influence in Christian higher education was also seen in the founding of the influential *Liberty University* in his hometown of Lynchburg, Virginia.[47] In response to the needs of women in crisis pregnancies, he also created the *Liberty Godparent Home*, a house which provides shelter and support to expectant mothers who have nowhere else to turn.[48]

The largest U. S. Baptist denomination, the *Southern Baptist Convention*, has also been very effective in moving public opinion in the pro-life direction. Even though the Southern Baptists originally approved of the 1973 *Roe v. Wade* decision, calling it an advance in the efforts for "religious liberty,"[49] in 1979 the denomination elected a conservative slate of officers, and passed a resolution supporting the passage of the Human Life Amendment.[50] This amendment sought to guarantee protection for the unborn in the U.S. Constitution. Since that time, the *Southern Baptist Convention* has been a prophetic voice in defense of the unborn, issuing numerous statements to educate its members and the public at large on the sanctity of life in the womb.

One of the most outspoken Southern Baptists on the national stage has been Richard D. Land, the president of the denomination's *Ethics and Religious Liberty Commission*. Land has written extensively on the subject of abortion, defended the sanctity of life on his weekly radio programs, and actively lobbied Congress to promote pro-life issues. An example of his lobbying efforts was his work to remove abortion coverage from bills being debated to reform the national health care system in 1994.[51]

44. Risen and Thomas, 127.

45. Ibid., 129.

46. Gorney, 346.

47. Risen and Thomas, 296.

48. Jacoby, 115.

49. John T. McGreevy, *Catholicism and American Freedom* (New York: W.W. Norton and Co., 2003), 262.

50. Gorney, 342.

51. Hendershott, 48.

CATHOLICS

Throughout the twentieth century, the doctrine of the Roman Catholic Church has remained consistently pro-life. Pope Pius XI (who reigned from 1920–1939) in his encyclical *Casti connubii,* rejected many of the excuses that were commonly offered to justify abortion.[52] Specifically, Pius XI refuted those who wanted to leave the abortion decision up to the parents, and those who worked to have abortion laws changed for medical, societal, or eugenic reasons.[53]

In 1951, Pope Pius XII, stated that human life was to be protected from the "first moment of its existence,"[54] meaning, of course, from the moment of conception. In an address given to the medical association *San Luca,* he emphasized the God-given dignity of the embryo, which therefore precluded the eugenic, social, and economic reasons that are often cited for performing abortions.[55]

The Catholic Church also actively defended the sanctity of human life during the second Vatican Council, which was held from 1962–1965. Before the beginning of the council, Pope John XXIII had already reiterated the Catholic Church's position against abortion in his encyclical *Mater et Magistra* (1961).[56] This was followed a few years later by the Vatican II document, *Gaudium et Spes,* in which the council fathers explained that abortion was "poisoning human society."[57] The encyclical also stated that "life from its conception is to be guarded with greatest care. Abortion and infanticide are horrible crimes."[58]

As support grew for legalized abortion during the late 1960s, Pope Paul VI responded by taking a strong stand against the practice in his 1968 encyclical *Humanae Vitae.*[59] In that work he writes, "In conformity with these landmarks in the human and Christian vision of marriage, we must once again declare that the direct interruption of the generative process

52. John Paul II, *The Gospel of Life.* (New York: Random House, 1995), 110.

53. Connery, 293.

54. Riddle, *Eve's Herbs,* 5–6.

55. John Paul II, *The Gospel of Life,* 111.

56. John W. Klotz, *A Christian View of Abortion.* (St. Louis, MO: Concordia Publishing House, 1973), 45.

57. Ficarra, 113.

58. Cited in Noonan, 45.

59. Kenneth D. Wald, *Religion and Politics in the United States.* (Washington, D.C.: CQ Press, 1992), 294.

already begun, and above all, directly willed and procured abortion, even if for therapeutic reasons, are to be absolutely excluded as licit means of regulating birth."[60] Paul VI also nailed down the Catholic Church's position on the abortion question by describing it as being consistent with historical doctrine and unchangeable as the Church proceeded into the future.[61]

In the 1960s, differences of opinion on the morality of contraception split Catholic moral theologians into two separate camps. It is notable that the contraception debate had little effect on the Catholic Church's opposition to abortion. In fact, the vast majority of those who favored liberalizing Catholic views on contraception, such as the aforementioned John T. Noonan (then a professor at Notre Dame), still maintained a strong pro-life stance on abortion.[62]

American Catholics can also take pride in the fact that their denomination took an active role in opposing the liberalization of abortion laws in the 1960s and 1970s. In 1972, the *United States Conference of Catholic Bishops* created its *Secretariat for Pro-Life Activities*, in response to new laws in many states which legalized abortion.[63] This new organization was headed up by Msgr. James McHugh, and it later became the secular *National Right to Life Committee*, which originally housed itself at the *National Council of Catholic Bishops (NCCB)* offices in Washington, D.C.[64] The *Secretariat for Pro-Life Activities* encouraged pro-life activism both at the state and federal levels. An example of state activism was Cardinal Terence Cook's leadership of a 1972 campaign which successfully reversed the 1970 abortion reform law in the New York state legislature. However, this reversal was later vetoed by Gov. Nelson Rockefeller.[65]

A day after the Supreme Court's *Roe v. Wade* decision of January 22, 1973, the *NCCB* issued a "Statement of the Committee of Pro-Life Affairs," which called the decision a "flagrant rejection of the unborn child's right to life."[66] It also called for legal challenges to the decision, and

60. Klotz, 45.

61. John Paul II, *The Gospel of Life*, 112.

62. Mc Greevy, 18.

63. Wald, 294.

64. Risen and Thomas, 19–20.

65. Ibid., 20.

66. Eva R. Rubin, ed., *The Abortion Controversy: A Documentary History*. (Westport CT: Greenwood Press, 1994), 141.

legislative action to limit abortion in the state legislatures. The statement also committed the Catholic Church's resources towards creating educational campaigns which would provide "scientific information on the humanity of the unborn child,"[67] and also reiterated Catholic hospitals' "dedication to the sanctity of human life."[68]

The *NCCB* also created a committee in late 1973 to lobby for the passage of the aforementioned Human Life Amendment.[69] Four U.S. cardinals actively lobbied Congress for the proposed amendment, and they testified before the Senate Judiciary committee on March 4, 1974.[70] One of the cardinals present at the Senate hearings, John Krol, the Archbishop of Philadelphia, stated,

> Last month, Mr. Justice Blackmun was quoted as saying that the court's abortion ruling 'will be regarded as one of the worst mistakes in the Court's history or one of its greatest decisions, a turning point.' I agree with Justice Blackmun at least to this extent, that the abortion decisions will be viewed as a tragic mistake. But I am convinced that they will ultimately be seen as the worst mistake in the Court's history. Only a constitutional amendment can correct this mistake.[71]

Later that same year, the Vatican's Sacred Congregation for the Doctrine of the Faith wrote a *Declaration on Abortion*, which once again reiterated that abortion was a violation of a human's right to life.[72]

During this time, many Catholics assumed leadership roles in the state and national right-to-life organizations that were created to lobby for laws which would once again protect the unborn.[73] This was a blessing and a curse, however, since the prominence of Catholics and the lack of Protestants in the pro-life movement led to a public perception that the

---

67. Rubin, ed., 142.

68. Ibid., 142.

69. Wald, 295.

70. Jean Garton, "Where are the Shepherds?" in *Back to the Drawing Board: The Future of the Pro-Life Movement,* ed. by Teresa R. Wagner (South Bend, IN: St. Augustine's Press, 2003), 230.

71. Rubin, ed., 191.

72. Ficarra, 113.

73. Wald, 294.

effort was outside the mainstream of American religious life, which was, and still is, predominantly Protestant.[74]

But despite the lack of support from its Protestant brethren, the Catholic Church continued efforts to reverse the effects of *Roe v. Wade* during the 1970s. In 1975, the *NCCB* created a *Pastoral Plan for Pro-Life Activities*, which included, along with other goals, a strategy to elect pro-life candidates to public office.[75] This effort was to be coordinated by "congressional district pro-life groups,"[76] which would not be "agenc[ies] of the church, nor . . . operated, controlled or financed by the church."[77] It was envisioned that these agencies would work with nonsectarian pro-life groups to convince legislators to vote for the Human Life Amendment.[78]

The *NCCB* also participated in a number of successful legislative efforts, such as the "conscience clause" law,[79] which prohibited hospitals from firing health care workers who refused to perform abortions.[80] It was also instrumental in the passage of the Hyde Amendment in 1976, named after its sponsor, pro-life Illinois congressman Henry Hyde. This amendment successfully prohibited Medicaid dollars from funding abortions, funds that had previously paid for 300,000 abortions in 1975.[81]

In fact, it is hard to underestimate the importance on the Catholic pro-life witness during the years immediately after *Roe*. In a paper used to testify before Congress in 1975, the *NCCB* boldly stated that, "No amount of statistical calculations, moral protestation or subtle legal argument can change the fact that an abortion destroys a human life . . . what moral principle can equitably and justly balance the potential accomplishment of social good with the direct and deliberate destruction of one million or more unborn human beings each year? There is no such principle."[82]

In 1981, the *NCCB* supported a compromise effort which it hoped would pass through the amendment process.[83] This amendment, named

74. Jacoby, 28.

75. Wald, 295.

76. Rubin, 222.

77. Ibid., 222.

78. Ibid., 222.

79. Risen and Thomas, 152.

80. Ibid., 17.

81. Ibid., 153.

82. Gorney, 238.

83. Ibid., 358.

the Hatch Amendment after its sponsor, Utah Senator Orrin Hatch, sought to simply guarantee the rights of Congress and the states to regulate abortion, since such regulation had largely been prohibited by *Roe*. It was, therefore, a watered-down version of the Human Life Amendment, which had sought to constitutionally guarantee the protection of the fetus from the moment of conception. The Hatch Amendment attempted to bring the law back to its previous status before *Roe*. It would then be up to each state to decide whether or not to allow abortion. But sadly, even this more moderate effort failed to pass through the amendment process.

> "Life before and after birth is like a seamless garment . . . . if we become insensitive to the beginning of life and condone abortion or if we become careless about the end of life and justify euthanasia, we have no reason to believe that there will be much respect for life in between."
>
> —Cardinal Bernardin

The election of Pope John Paul II in 1978 brought a great champion of the unborn to the pontificate. On his first visit to the United States in 1979, the Pope spoke in front of the Lincoln memorial in Washington, D.C. and asked that Americans "defend human life against every influence or action that threatens or weakens it."[84] John Paul II's 1995 encyclical *Evangelium Vitae*, reaffirmed Pope Paul VI's encyclical *Humanae Vitae*, while updating that vision for the end of the twentieth century. He wrote, "We are facing an enormous and drastic clash between good and evil, death and life, the 'culture of death' and the 'culture of life.'"[85] Speaking specifically on the abortion issue he stated, "Among all the crimes which can be committed against life, procured abortion has characteristics making it particularly serious and deplorable."[86] In speaking out against euphemisms which were used to describe abortion, such as referring to an abortion as an "interruption of pregnancy," he said, "procured abortion is *the deliberate and direct killing, by whatever means*

---

84. McGreevy, 281.

85. John Paul II, *The Gospel of Life*, 50.

86. Ibid., 103.

it is carried out, of a human being in the initial phase of his or her existence, extending from conception to birth." [italics original][87]

In his book *Crossing the Threshold of Hope*, John Paul II also elaborated on the responsibility that the Christian community had in supporting women who found themselves in crisis pregnancies. He states,

> therefore in firmly rejecting 'pro-choice' it is necessary to become courageously 'pro-woman,' promoting a choice that is truly in favor of women. It is precisely the woman, in fact, who pays the highest price, not only for her motherhood, but even more for its destruction, for the suppression of the life of the child who has been conceived. The only honest stance, in these cases, is that of radical solidarity with the woman. It is not right to leave her alone. The experience of many counseling centers shows that the woman does not want to suppress the life of the child she carries within her. If she is supported in this attitude, and if at the same time she is freed from the intimidation of those around her, then she is even capable of heroism.[88]

The broad consensus in the 1980s within the Catholic Church on the issue of abortion included liberal clerics such as Chicago Archbishop Joseph Cardinal Bernardin (a strong advocate of nuclear disarmament in the 1980s),[89] as well as conservative leaders such as the late John Cardinal O'Connor of New York. Bernadin, who headed the *National Council of Catholic Bishops* in 1983,[90] and many of his contemporary Catholics on the political left saw the pro-life movement and its concern for the unborn to be consistent with Christian social justice teachings. He wrote, "a decision to deny protection to human life in the early stages of its development must be judged arbitrary and inadequate."[91] He also stated, "Life before and after birth is like a seamless garment . . . . if we become insensitive to the beginning of life and condone abortion or if we become careless about the end of life and justify euthanasia, we have no reason to believe that there will be much respect for life in between."[92]

---

87. John Paul II, *The Gospel of Life*, 103.

88. Cited in Jacoby, 169.

89. Ficarra, 102.

90. Risen and Thomas, 65.

91. Cited in Ficarra, 102.

92. Cited in Doerflinger, Richard M. "The Pro-Life Message and Catholic Social Teaching: Problems of Reception," in *American Catholics, American Culture, Traditions*

Bernardin was not alone in seeing the pro-life movement as an integral component of a comprehensive effort for social justice. In fact, the Catholic Church has made the right to life a social justice priority that is the foundation for all other human rights. In *Living the Gospel of Life: A Challenge to American Catholics*, the *U.S. Conference of Catholic Bishops* wrote, "Indeed, the failure to protect and defend life in its most vulnerable stages renders suspect any claims to the 'rightness' of positions in other matters effecting the poorest and least powerful of the human community."[93]

John Cardinal O'Connor of New York City also took up the effort to support "the poorest and least powerful of the human community" by pledging to care for any woman who could not afford to pay the medical expenses to bring her child to term. He wrote,

> I announced on Oct. 15, 1984 and many times since then, and even
> if people get tired of hearing me say it, I will keep saying it and
> saying it again: *Any* woman, of any color, of any age, of any reli-
> gion, who is pregnant and in need can come to the Archdiocese of
> New York, can come to me personally, can call me, can come to our
> Catholic Charities. We will take complete care of her, free of charge.
> We will help her to keep her baby if she wishes to keep the baby. We
> will help her to have the baby adopted if that is what she wishes. We
> will provide medical and hospital care. We will give her the support
> and encouragement she needs to take away her fear.[94]

Cardinal O'Connor also pointed out that the medical community, if it so desired, could quickly end the nation's epidemic of abortion. He wrote, "This point warrants repetition: if doctors, in accord with the Hippocratic oath [which contains an explicit prohibition on abortion] wanted to eliminate abortion, they could do so almost entirely because they are the persons who perform the overwhelming number of abortions. Medical schools and medical societies must become target areas for reeducation on the dignity of all human life."[95]

---

and Resistance, ed. by Margaret O'Brien Steinfels (New York: Rowman and Littlefield, 2004), 53.

93. Doerflinger, 54.

94. John Cardinal O'Connor, "Commemoration of the Twentieth Anniversary of *Roe vs. Wade*," in *The Right Choice*, ed. by Paul T. Stallsworth (Nashville, TN: Abingdon Press, 1997), 73–74.

95. Ficarra, 102.

Unlike most of its Protestant counterparts, the Catholic Church has also been willing to discipline those who have openly contradicted its teachings on abortion. On October 7, 1984, *Catholics for a Free Choice* published a full-page advertisement in the *New York Times* which stated that the Church's views on abortion were not the final word for Catholics, and that they had the right to follow their own consciences on the matter. The advertisement was also signed by many Catholics, but most notably, by a number of priests and nuns who were active in ministry in the Catholic Church. The Holy See responded strongly to the signatures of these clergy members, noting that these clerics had caused "flagrant scandal." The Vatican also requested public recantations from all the signatories, and threatened that they could be "dismissed from the religious life."[96]

Many commentators have questioned why Catholics and Protestants responded differently to abortion legalization efforts in the 1960s and 1970s. John Klotz, a former professor at Concordia University-River Forest, theorizes that the willingness of the Catholic Church to lobby for abortion laws may come from its belief that it is the natural law, and not just the Christian faith, which renders abortion immoral. And since abortion is a violation of the natural law, the Catholic Church believes that the prohibition against abortion applies to every nation, whether it is Christian or not.[97] Therefore, this belief in the natural law may explain the Catholic willingness to lobby for laws against abortion, and the reticence of some Protestant denominations which do not believe in the natural law.

Klotz also believes that this Catholic "natural law" perspective differs from the "two kingdoms" view of Lutherans and many other Protestants. The "two kingdoms" view recognizes two kingdoms in society: the kingdom of the state and the kingdom of the church. The kingdom of the state wields the authority of civil justice and holds the "power of the sword" (Romans 13), which is the authority to mete out civil punishment—and even capital punishment—on those who disobey the law. The kingdom of the church, on the other hand, has authority over spiritual matters. This theology also teaches that civil authorities cannot control against all violations of divine law, nor can they demand fidelity to Christian morality from an often non-Christian populace. Klotz has suggested that the "two kingdoms approach holds that a civil government can only be expected to

---

96. Ficarra, 105–7.

97. Klotz, 46.

police the more injurious violations of a society's moral code which pose a direct threat to peace and order."[98]

With such a theology, many Protestant denominations may have believed that abortion should not be prohibited by the civil authorities just because it was a violation of God's law. And while it is important to understand that many Protestants, including Dr. James Lamb, the executive director of *Lutherans for Life*, have successfully refuted this misconception of the "two kingdoms" theology with regard to abortion, one cannot dismiss the effect this view has had in dampening the Protestant pro-life movement.

In 1992, the Supreme Court case *Casey v. Planned Parenthood* held out hope in Catholic pro-life circles, and in the pro-life community at large, that the nineteen year-old *Roe v. Wade* decision might be reversed. Sadly, by a 5 to 4 decision, the court upheld *Roe*, and also tried to inject religion into the decision by stating that each person should be able to "define one's own concept of existence, of meaning, of the universe, and of the mystery of human life."[99] This portion of the majority opinion, which was later coined the "mystery passage," deeply insulted millions of faithful Americans when it transparently used quasi-religious language to legitimatize abortion-on-demand.

One of the most powerful critics of the Supreme Court within the Catholic Church has been the Catholic priest and editor of *First Things* magazine, Richard John Neuhaus. In regard to the "mystery passage," Neuhaus wrote, "the justices wax theological about the mystery of human life in total disregard of precisely that, the mystery of human life. For the Supreme Court, the mystery of human life is to be defined by the individual; but for most [Christians], the mystery of human life is discovered as a gift. For the Court, authentic personhood requires freedom from an encumbering community; but for most of us, to be a person is to be a person in community."[100]

The Catholic Church's doctrine on the immorality of abortion was further clarified in its 1994 *Catechism of the Catholic Church*. The catechism makes three points on the subject. First, it explains that abortion is a grave violation of divine and natural law, and pronounces the pun-

---

98. Klotz, 55.

99. Cited in Richard John Neuhaus, "The Religion of the Sovereign Self," in *The Right Choice*, ed. by Paul T. Stallsworth (Nashville, TN: Abingdon Press, 1997), 63–64.

100. Ibid., 64.

ishment of excommunication for the offense. Nevertheless, it also offers forgiveness through the sacrament of confession. The *Catechism* states,

> Formal cooperation in an abortion constitutes a grave offense. The Church attaches the canonical penalty of excommunication to this crime against human life. 'A person who procures a completed abortion incurs excommunication *latae sententiae*,'[76] 'by the very commission of the offense,'[77] and subject to the conditions provided by Canon Law.[78] The Church does not thereby intend to restrict the scope of mercy. Rather, she makes clear the gravity of the crime committed, the irreparable harm done to the innocent who is put to death, as well as to the parents and the whole of society.[101] [footnote citations provided in Appendix I]

Secondly, the *Catechism* explains that the act of abortion is a violation of an unborn child's basic human rights, as well as a violation of the Christian commandment to "love one another." It says,

> The inalienable right to life of every innocent human individual is a constitutive element of a civil society and its legislation: The inalienable rights of the person must be recognized and respected by civil society and the political authority. These human rights depend neither on single individuals nor on parents; nor do they represent a concession made by society and the state; they belong to human nature and are inherent in the person by virtue of the creative act from which the person took his origin. Among such fundamental rights one should mention in this regard every human being's right to life and physical integrity from the moment of conception until death.[79][102] [footnote citations provided in Appendix I]

Thirdly, in the *Catechism* the Catholic Church reiterates its belief that civil governments have a duty to protect the unborn by creating laws which outlaw abortion. As stated before, this belief is based on the natural law and on Catholic social justice teachings which recognize society's responsibility to care for the disenfranchised, the vulnerable, and the downtrodden. The *Catechism* states,

> The moment a positive law deprives a category of human beings of the protection which civil legislation ought to accord them, the state is denying the equality of all before the law. When the state

---

101. *Catechism of the Catholic Church.* (New Hope, KY: Urbi et Orbi Communications, 1994), 548.

102. Ibid., 548.

does not place its power at the service of the rights of each citizen, and in particular of the more vulnerable, the very foundations of a state based on law are undermined . . . As a consequence of the respect and protection which must be ensured for the unborn child from the moment of conception, the law must provide appropriate penal sanctions for every deliberate violation of the child's rights.[80][103] [footnote citations provided in Appendix I]

In the same vein, the *Catechism* also states, "Because it should be treated as a person from conception, the embryo must be defended in its integrity, cared for and healed like every other human being."[104]

In addition to being a decade when the Catholic Church more fully explained its position on the sinfulness of abortion, the 1990s, were also a decade in which Catholics defended the rights of healthcare workers to refuse to participate in abortion services. The most notable effort in this area was the work of the *Catholic Health Association*, which lobbied successfully to stop local jurisdictional requirements which would have required abortion training in Catholic hospitals.[105]

Since the 1960s, the Catholic Church has also been blessed by a number of priests who have had the opportunity to work in the pro-life ministry. One such priest is the aforementioned Father Richard John Neuhaus, who became a recognized commentator on pro-life issues after the publication of his highly influential article "Abortion: The Dangerous Assumptions," in the June 1967 issue of *Commonweal* magazine. In reading this article, one is struck with the similarity of arguments for and against abortion in the 1960s and arguments used by pro-choice and pro-life activists today. For example, Neuhaus discusses the confusing rhetoric of abortion, the lack of distinction between abortion and contraception, the incidence of post-abortion syndrome, whether the legalization of abortion was a worse evil than the elimination of unsafe illegal abortions, and what he calls "middle class smugness."[106]

---

103. *Catechism of the Catholic Church*, 548.

104. Ibid., 558.

105. C. Joffe, et al., "Pro-Choice Medical Activism," in *Abortion Wars: A Half Century of Struggle 1950–2000*, ed. by Rickie Solinger (Berkeley: University of California Press, 1998), 326.

106. Richard John Neuhaus, "Abortion: The Dangerous Assumptions," *Commonweal*. 30 June 1967, 411.

This last attitude is the tendency of pro-choicers to advocate abortions for poor mothers. Neuhaus gives the example of a pro-choice physician who testifies at a legislative hearing that only those children who have "a stable home with a responsible father in the house, adequate income to share the necessities and a chance for higher education, [and] an accepting attitude where [the child] would not be looked upon as an intrusion"[107] ought to be kept full-term. Neuhaus notes that by that definition the majority of children in his Brooklyn congregation should not even be alive![108]

Neuhaus also uses his experience as an activist in the civil rights movement to argue that it is the pro-life, rather than the pro-choice position, which is consistent with the fight for social justice. This is because the pro-life ministry seeks to expand the human community, and also expand the care that human beings provide for one another. In Neuhaus's view, the practice of abortion can, by its very nature, only restrict the community.[109] He also explains that the pro-life movement needs to serve those who feel they have no other choice besides abortion, and he urges ecumenical efforts to assist unwed mothers and provide adoption services. He ends the article by arguing for a less judgmental attitude by the church toward unwed mothers.[110]

Neuhaus was highly influenced by Methodist ethicist and Princeton professor Paul Ramsey, who invited him to participate as a board member in the pro-life legal organization, *Americans United for Life*.[111] Interestingly, Neuhaus is a convert from the Lutheran faith, and while a Lutheran pastor he strongly supported the creation of *Lutherans For Life* in 1978. But he is probably best known in the right-to-life movement for the many pro-life articles he has written in *First Things*, a religion and culture magazine which he started in 1990.[112]

Another great Catholic advocate of the unborn during the 1970s was Father Paul Marx. In 1971, after attending the *California Abortion Sym-*

---

107. Richard John Neuhaus, "Abortion: The Dangerous Assumptions," 411.

108. Ibid., 411.

109. Richard John Neuhaus, telephone and e-mail interview with the author, September 11 and 13, 2007.

110. Richard John Neuhaus, "Abortion: The Dangerous Assumptions," 413.

111. Richard John Neuhaus, telephone and e-mail interview with the author, September 11 and 13, 2007.

112. Ibid.

posium (using the pseudonym "Dr. Paul Marx"), which included graphic discussions of abortion procedures,[113] he wrote the book, *Death Peddlars: War on the Unborn*, an exposé on the abortion industry.[114]

The Symposium featured such speakers as the Rev. J. Hugh Anwyl, a member of the *Clergy Consultation Service*; Senator Bob Packwood of Oregon, who spoke on legislative efforts to legalize abortion across the nation; and Dr. Joseph F. Fletcher, who at that time was a professor of medical ethics at the University of Virginia.[115] Dr. Fletcher, who presented himself as an ethical guide to the abortion doctors and nurses present at the symposium, shared many of the previously discussed theological misconceptions about abortion.[116] But most importantly, *Death Peddlars* allowed the public to see the sordid reality of abortion procedures and the radical views of abortion practitioners, and it cut through the rhetoric of "choice" as few books had before.

> "In giving His Body, Christ teaches the meaning of love. I sacrifice myself for the good of the other person. Abortion teaches the opposite of love: I sacrifice the other person for the good of myself!"
>
> –Rev. Frank Pavone

Marx's efforts also included the creation of the *Human Life Center* in 1972 at St. John's University in Collegeville, Minnesota.[117] And in 1981, he started the pro-life organization *Human Life International*, which currently has its headquarters in Front Royal, Virginia, and is active in pro-life ministry in over forty countries around the world.[118]

Another strong Catholic leader in the pro-life movement is Father Frank Pavone. Ordained in the Archdiocese on New York in 1988 by the aforementioned Cardinal O'Connor, Pavone became the National Director

---

113. "Our Founder - The Rev. Paul Marx, OSB" in Human Life International website. (Front Royal, VA, 12 October, 2002 [cited 24 August 2007]); available from http://www.hli.org/rev_paul_marx_tribute.html; INTERNET.

114. Paul Marx, *Death Peddlars: War on the Unborn*. (Collegeville, MN: St. John's University Press, 1971), 4.

115. Ibid., 188–190.

116. Ibid., 162–163.

117. "Our Founder - The Rev. Paul Marx, OSB."

118. Ibid.

of *Priests for Life* in 1993.[119] That organization had been created three years before by Father Lee Kaylor, a priest in the diocese of San Francisco, who saw the need to create an organization which would encourage priests in the Bay Area to preach on the sanctity of human life.[120] Under Pavone's leadership, *Priests for Life* grew to become a powerful international pro-life voice. He has also been tireless in his efforts to educate the Catholic community on the sanctity of life, traveling to all fifty states and five continents.[121]

Pavone, along with Janet Morana, the Associate Director of *Priests for Life*, hosts the *Defending Life* television program on the *Eternal Word Television Network*, the *Gospel of Life* television show on *Sky Angel* television, and the *Life on the Line* radio show on Salem and Bott radio. He is also president of the *National Pro-Life Religious Council*, an organization devoted to affirming the pro-life message of Christianity, and is also the chairman of the board of *Rachel's Vineyard*, a healing retreat ministry for those who have experienced abortion.[122] In 2004, Pavone started a pro-life Catholic religious order called the *Missionaries of the Gospel of Life* in the diocese of Amarillo, Texas.

> "How do we persuade a woman not to have an abortion? As always, we must persuade her with love, and we remind ourselves that love means to be willing to give until it hurts. Jesus gave even His life to love us. So, the mother who is thinking of abortion should be helped to love, that is, to give until it hurts her plans, or her free time, to respect the life of her child. The father of that child, whoever he is, must also give until it hurts."
>
> —Mother Theresa

Pavone was also active in efforts to elect pro-life candidates during the 2000 and 2004 national elections. His brochure, "Voting with a Clear Conscience," explains that the most important issue facing the voters

---

119. "Father Frank A. Pavone - Biography," in Priests for Life website. (Staten Island, NY 2007 [cited 3 July 2007]); available from http://www.priestsforlife.org/intro/ffbio.html; INTERNET.

120. Anthony Desteffano, "How Did Priests for Life Start?" *Priests for Life Newsletter*, vol. 11, Number 1, January–February 2001, 1.

121. "Father Frank A. Pavone—Biography," in Priests for Life website.

122. Ibid.

during those elections is the right to life.[123] He is also author of the 2006 book, *Ending Abortion, Not Just Fighting It,* which provides Christians with practical advice on how to change hearts on the abortion issue.[124] In the book, Pavone powerfully[125] contrasts Jesus's view of the body with the pro-choice view of the body,

> Did you ever realize that the same four words that were used by the Lord Jesus to save the world are also used by some to promote abortion? "This Is My Body." The same simple words are spoken from opposite ends of the universe, with meanings that are directly contrary to each other.
>
> When the Lord Jesus took bread, blessed it, broke it, and gave it to His disciples, saying, 'This is my Body, which is given up for you,' He was pointing to what would happen the next day, when He would give that same body on the cross. He sacrifices Himself so that we may live. He gives up His body so that He can destroy the power of sin and death. As a result, He welcomes us into His life, into His Kingdom. He makes us members of His Body!
>
> On the other hand, abortion supporters say, "This is my body. So don't interfere with it! It's mine, so I can do what I want, even to the point of killing the life within it. All is secondary to my dominion over my body." In fact one abortion supporter has written, "I say their (pro-lifer's) God is worth nothing compared to my body" (Michelle Goldberg, 'Rant for Choice,' in University of Buffalo student newspaper, 1995).
>
> "This is my body." Same words, different results. Christ gives His body away so others might live; abortion supporters cling to their own bodies so others might die. In giving His Body, Christ teaches the meaning of love. I sacrifice myself for the good of the other person. Abortion teaches the opposite of love: I sacrifice the other person for the good of myself![126]

Another prominent Catholic defender of the unborn was Mother Teresa. A great missionary to the poor and afflicted in the most desti-

123. Frank Pavone, e-mail interview with the author, September 22, 2007.

124. Ibid.

125. Author's note: I have seen Father Pavone preach many times, and it is in this context that one sees his true passion for the unborn. Addressing his listeners as "Brothers and Sisters," and sharing the gospel of life with a powerful style, he reminds one of a Baptist preacher. And it is in this manner that Father Pavone resonates with all Christian audiences, both Catholic and Protestant.

126. Frank Pavone, *Ending Abortion, Not Just Fighting It.* (Totowa, NJ: Catholic Book Publishing Company, 2006), 178.

tute neighborhoods of Calcutta, India, her defense of the downtrodden naturally extended to the womb as well. At the 1994 National Prayer Breakfast in Washington, D.C., Mother Teresa had this to say about life and abortion,

> How do we persuade a woman not to have an abortion? As always, we must persuade her with love, and we remind ourselves that love means to be willing to give until it hurts. Jesus gave even His life to love us. So, the mother who is thinking of abortion should be helped to love, that is, to give until it hurts her plans, or her free time, to respect the life of her child. The father of that child, whoever he is, must also give until it hurts.[127]

And at the same talk, Mother Teresa made a plea to those considering abortion,

> Please don't kill the child. I want the child. Please give me the child. I am willing to accept any child who would be aborted and to give that child to a married couple who will love the child and be loved by the child. From our children's home in Calcutta alone, we have saved over three thousand children from abortion. These children have brought such love and joy to their adopting parents and have grown up so full of love and joy.[128]

CONGREGATIONALISTS

The largest Congregational denomination in the United States, the *United Church of Christ (UCC)*, can safely be described as being staunchly pro-choice. In its latest position statement on abortion, which can be found in Appendix I, the *UCC* totally ignores the rights of the unborn and instead concentrates solely on its belief that the mother should have a completely unencumbered right to procure an abortion.

The denomination began its move towards the pro-choice position in the late 1960s and early 1970s when an increasing number of its clergy members became active participants in the *Clergy Consultation Service*.[129] In 1970, the denomination made its first official move towards the

---

127. Mother Teresa of Calcutta, "Whatever You Did unto One of the Least, You Did unto Me," in *The Right Choice*, ed. by Paul T. Stallsworth (Nashville, TN: Abingdon Press, 1997), 104.

128. Ibid., 106.

129. John B. Brown and Robin Fox, eds. *Affirming Life: Biblical Perspectives on*

pro-choice position when the *United Church Board of Homeland Ministries* (*UCBHM*) and the *Council for Christian Social Action* voted for the reform of laws which prohibited abortion.[130] The next year, at its 1971 Eighth General Synod, the denomination passed a "Freedom of Choice Concerning Abortion" proposal by a 523 to 51 delegate vote.[131] Although outnumbered, there was still a vocal group of pro-life delegates at the synod, and the Rev. Robert M. Bartlett delivered a powerful speech against the proposal.[132] But the *UCC's* pro-choice activism continued in 1973, when the *UCBHM* provided amicus briefs to the U.S. Supreme Court in support of the pro-choice petition in the famous *Roe v. Wade* case, and the *UCBHM*, along with the *UCC Office of Church in Society* became founding members of *RCAR* (later *RCRC*).[133]

> "Often with regard to *abortion*, euphemisms are used in place of the word abortion and the phrase *unborn child. Abortion*, in the pro–choice vocabulary becomes *cleaning out of the uterus, emptying of the uterus*, or *termination of pregnancy*. Likewise, *unborn child* becomes *fetus* (used in a pejorative sense), *garbage, parasite, product of conception, protoplasmic mass*, or *subhuman piece of tissue*."
>
> –Rev. John Brown

At the 1977 synod which was held in Washington, D.C., a renewal group called *United Church People for Biblical Witness* was created in reaction to the *UCC's* acceptance of a human sexuality study which further liberalized the denomination's views on abortion.[134] Headed by *UCC* pastor's wife (and later attorney) Barbara Weller, this organization changed its name to *Biblical Witness Fellowship* in 1985.[135]

When the need for a stronger pro-life presence was recognized within the denomination, *Biblical Witness Fellowship* created *UCC Friends for*

Abortion for the United Church of Christ. (Princeton, NJ: Princeton University Press, 1991), 26.

130. Brown and Fox, eds., 26.

131. Ibid., 26.

132. Ibid., 29.

133. Ibid., 27.

134. John Brown, telephone interview by the author, September 10, 2007.

135. Ibid.

Life (UCCFFL) in 1984 to educate its faithful on the life issues.[136] This new organization was organized by two *UCC* pastor's wives, Connie Carmany, R.N. and Dr. Gretchen Wagner[137] at a *United Church People for Biblical Witness* convention in Byfield, Massachusetts.[138] *UCC Friends for Life* was later accepted as an interest group of the *UCC* in 1985.[139]

Over the years, this organization has actively lobbied the U.S. Supreme Court, providing friend of the court briefs for the *Webster v. Reproductive Health Services* (1988), *Turnock v. Ragsdale* (1989), and *Rust v. Sullivan* (1990) cases,[140] and has diligently worked to educate *UCC* members on the life issues. *UCC Friends for Life* also started *Loving Touch Ministries* which works to teach congregations how to support women in crisis pregnancies.[141] The Rev. John Brown, formerly the president of the *NPRC*, and since 1990 the president of the *UCC Friends for Life*, has defended the sanctity of life within his denomination for nearly three decades. His ministry has also unveiled the euphemisms that have been used to support the pro-choice position. He writes,

> Often with regard to abortion, euphemisms are used in place of the word *abortion* and the phrase *unborn child*. *Abortion*, in the pro-choice vocabulary becomes *cleaning out of the uterus, emptying of the uterus*, or *termination of pregnancy*. Likewise, *unborn child* becomes *fetus* (used in a pejorative sense), *garbage, parasite, product of conception, protoplasmic mass*, or *subhuman piece of tissue*. Considering these substitutions, you can easily see that the purpose behind their usage is distortion and deception. They are used to cover up what is in fact taking place in abortion: the destruction of a child, the destruction of over 20 million children who were created in the image and likeness of God . . . The truth is, every human being—no matter how young, no matter how helpless, is a human being. The truth is, every human being is created by God, through the natural workings of conception. The truth is, every human being is one for whom Christ died. Therefore, every human being is worthy of our respect. [italics original][142]

136. John Brown, telephone interview by the author, September 10, 2007.

137. "Landmarks in UCC Renewal," *The Witness*. Winter 2004, 16.

138. John B. Brown and Robin Fox, eds., 29.

139. Ibid., 29.

140. Ibid., 29.

141. Ibid., 82.

142. John B. Brown, "Rejoicing in the Truth," in *The Right Choice*, ed. by Paul T.

Even though the *UCC* leadership has done little to promote the sanctity of human life, the Congregational tradition includes other denominations which have taken up the pro-life banner. For instance, the *Conservative Congregational Christian Conference (CCCC)*, has remained firmly pro-life, and has actively promoted the pro-life cause in its churches. Its sanctity of life ministry has been most recently led by the Rev. Jan Kirk van der Swaagh, who became active in the pro-life movement during the abortion clinic "rescue" protests of the late 1980s.[143] Besides educating *CCCC* churches on the life issues, van der Swaagh also serves as the Vice President of the *NPRC*.[144]

Another noteworthy pro-life Congregationalist minister was the aforementioned Harold O. J. Brown, who co-founded *Care Net* in 1975.[145] Over his career as a pastor and seminary professor, Brown authored numerous pro-life articles, but he is probably best known for his groundbreaking 1977 book, *Death Before Life*. This book, which was one of the first pro-life books authored by a Protestant minister after *Roe v. Wade*, testified about the Christian responsibility to speak out in obedience to God's moral law on behalf of the unborn. It states, "The answer seems obvious: it is our responsibility to warn our fellow Christians and our fellow Americans of the danger of death that comes with transgression of God's moral law. If they will not hear, that is *their* responsibility. If we fail to tell them, it is *ours*."[italics original][146]

EPISCOPALIANS

As late as 1958, the Lambeth Conference of the worldwide Anglican Communion stated that abortion was the "killing of life already conceived."[147] However, changing views in the 1960s surrounding the abortion question shifted many Protestant opinions on the subject, with the Episcopal Church affirming a limited pro-choice position at its Seattle, WA

Stallsworth (Nashville, TN: Abingdon Press, 1997), 38–39.

143. Jan Kirk van der Swaagh, e-mail interview by the author, October 15, 2007.

144. Ibid.

145. Authors note: I had the privilege of having Dr. Brown as my thesis advisor at *Reformed Theological Seminary* in Charlotte, NC., and he was indeed a passionate and highly erudite advocate of the unborn.

146. Harold O.J. Brown, *Death Before Birth*. (New York: Thomas Nelson Inc. Publishers, 1977), 162–63.

147. Gorman and Brooks, 56.

general convention of 1967. The convention voted to support "abortion-law reform, to permit the termination of pregnancy, where the decision to terminate has been arrived at with proper safeguards against abuse, and where it has been clearly established that the physical or mental health of the mother is threatened seriously, or where there is substantial reason to believe that the child would be born badly deformed in mind or body, or where the pregnancy has resulted from rape or incest."[148] However, the convention also clearly condemned abortions which were performed for the following reasons: "Because the birth of a child would be inconvenient or socially embarrassing, because the child was conceived out of wedlock, because the mother is under fifteen, because the pregnancy might prove difficult, or because the family cannot afford a baby."[149]

At its 1976 convention, three years after the *Roe v. Wade* decision, the denomination reaffirmed its previous 1967 convention position, but strengthened its pro-choice stance by stating "that in those cases where it is firmly and deeply believed by the person or persons concerned that pregnancy should be terminated for causes other than the above [see 1967 statement above], members of this church are urged to seek the advice and counsel of a Priest of this church . . ."[150] But it also strictly opposed abortions performed for "convenience."[151]

At its 1982 convention, the Episcopal Church included a number of limitations on abortions. It stated that it "strongly condemns the act of abortion when the sole purpose of such action is the selection of the sex of the child."[152] It added that, "abortion in a case where purely cosmetic abnormalities are discovered, is also strongly condemned."[153]

Yet despite these limitations, the Episcopal Church's position on abortion only became more radical as the years progressed, and it even opposed legislative efforts to obtain parental consent for abortions for

---

148. General Convention, *Journal of the General Convention of the Protestant Episcopal Church, 1967* (New York: Protestant Episcopal Press, 1968), 308.

149. Ibid., 307.

150. General Convention, *Journal of the General Convention of the Protestant Episcopal Church, 1976* (New York: Protestant Episcopal Press, 1977), C-3.

151. Ibid., C-3.

152. General Convention, *Journal of the General Convention of the Protestant Episcopal Church, 1982* (New York: Protestant Episcopal Press, 1983), C-157.

153. Ibid., C-157.

minors at its 1991 convention.[154] In addition, at its 1994 convention it passed what became known as its "unequivocal opposition" clause. This clause strengthened the wording of its previous statements, and expressed the denomination's "unequivocal opposition to any legislative, executive, or judicial action on the part of local, state or national government that abridges the right of a woman to reach an informed decision about termination of pregnancy or that would limit the access of a woman to safe means of acting on her decision."[155] This "unequivocal opposition" to any legal limitation on abortion was vividly demonstrated when the Presiding Bishop of the Episcopal Church sent a letter of support to President Clinton after his veto of the *Partial-Birth Abortion Ban Act* of 1995.[156]

Despite the often extreme pro-choice positions of the American Episcopal Church, many Episcopalians have actively defended the unborn. In response to state laws being passed in the 1960s that legalized abortion, the Rt. Rev. Joseph M. Harte of the Diocese of Arizona founded the group *Episcopalians for Life* in 1966,[157] which organized chapters around the country to educate the Episcopalian community on the sanctity of life.[158] On December 6, 1983, that organization reorganized under a new name, *The National Organization of Episcopalians for Life Research and Education Foundation,* or *NOEL,* and the Rt. Rev. John Howe, then of Truro Church in Fairfax, Virginia, was named its chairman of the board.[159] From 1983 to 1986, *NOEL* worked out of offices in Fairfax, with the goal of passing pro-life resolutions at the national Episcopal general

---

154. General Convention, *Journal of the General Convention of the Protestant Episcopal Church, Phoenix 1991* (New York: Domestic and Foreign Missionary Society of the Protestant Episcopal Church in the USA, 1992), 839.

155. General Convention, *Journal of the General Convention of . . . The Episcopal Church, Indianapolis, 1994* (New York: General Convention, 1995), 324–25.

156. "HR 1833 and the United Church of Christ," in the Worldwide faith News website (New York, 20 May 1996 [cited 31 December 2007]); available from http://www.wfn.org/1996/05/msg00749.html; INTERNET.

157. "History and Overview of Anglicans for Life," in Anglicans for Life website. (Sewickley, PA, 2007 [cited 25 June 2007]); available from http://www.anglicansforlife.org/about/history.asp; INTERNET.

158. Ibid.

159. Ibid.

conventions.[160] In 1996, *NOEL* was relocated to Sewickly, Pennsylvania, and in 1998, it elected its fifth president, Georgette Forney.[161]

In 2001, NOEL made inroads into parish pro-life education by starting the *Parish Point Person Program*. This program assisted pro-life parishioners by providing sanctity of life resources to local dioceses and churches.[162] In 2002, along with *Priests for Life*, NOEL started the *Silent No More Awareness Campaign*, "to educate the public that abortion physically, emotionally, and spiritually hurts women, men, and others involved."[163] Since that time, *Silent No More* has held numerous demonstrations around the country. Each rally has given post-abortive women the opportunity to hold signs which state, "I Regret My Abortion," and also the forum to openly testify to the devastating effect that abortion has had on their lives.[164] In addition, the group has gained national publicity through its celebrity spokesperson, the actress Jennifer O'Neill.

NOEL has also educated the Episcopal Church on the life issues through its monthly magazine "NewsBrief," and through Ms. Forney's 2007 book, *Why Life Is Important*.[165] Due to the disassociation of many U.S. Episcopal churches from their dioceses in response to the ordination of an openly gay bishop in New Hampshire, *NOEL* changed its name to *Anglicans for Life* in 2006.[166]

While Episcopalians have been blessed with a strong pro-life organization here in the United States, they have also been encouraged by the fact that the leader of the worldwide Anglican Communion, the Archbishop of Canterbury Rowan Williams, has remained outspokenly pro-life. A life-long member of the British *Society for the Protection of Unborn Children*, he has stated that "from the moment of conception there is a moral other involved."[167] Archbishop Williams has also stated that "abortion is the taking of human life."[168]

160. "History and Overview of Anglicans for Life."

161. Ibid.

162. Ibid.

163. Ibid.

164. Ibid.

165. Georgette Forney, e-mail interview by the author, October 5, 2007.

166. "History and Overview of Anglicans for Life."

167. Gorman and Brooks, 58.

168. Ibid., 58.

While a change in the pro-choice stance of the Episcopal Church's leadership may be decades away, the smaller *Charismatic Episcopal Church (CEC)* has been very active on behalf of the unborn. In fact, that denomination's patriarch, Randolph Adler, has been involved in the pro-life movement since the 1980s, when he was imprisoned numerous times for participating in peaceful protests against abortion.[169] In the year 2000, the *CEC's* House of Bishops approved the creation of a pro-life ministry called *CEC for Life* to educate its churches on the life issues, and in 1992 the denomination approved a *Declaration on the Sanctity of Human Life* (see Appendix I), which reaffirmed its strong defense of the preborn.[170]

Today, *CEC for Life* is headed by its director, Father Terry Gensemer, who hopes to see its efforts culminating in the "rehumanizing of the preborn and the restoration of the God-ordained fact that children in the womb are made in the image of God."[171] The organization also works with the Irish pro-life organization *Youth Defence*, and coordinates an annual educational trip to Ireland with the denomination's pro-life youth group, *Laudate for Life*.[172] *CEC for Life* has also written a *Liturgy for the Pre-Born at the Time of Death*, which has been celebrated numerous times in front of abortion clinics.[173]

LUTHERANS

In the late 1960s, the denominations which would, in 1988, merge to become the *Evangelical Lutheran Church of America (ELCA)*, changed their doctrine to allow abortion. *ELCA's* decision to accept the morality of abortion was a clear break from traditional Lutheranism. That tradition was staunchly pro-life, as we have previously shown with the quote from Martin Luther in chapter 5. But *ELCA's* pro-choice position was also more moderate than those of its mainline brethren, and its social teaching statement which passed at its 1991 Churchwide Assembly in Orlando, Florida, stated that an abortion after viability was sinful. It also encour-

---

169. Terry Gensemer, telephone interview by author, July 30, 2007.

170. Ibid.

171. Ibid.

172. Ibid.

173. Ibid.

aged adoption as a "positive option" to abortion, and further stated that "Abortion ought to be an option of only last resort."[174]

But despite the *ELCA*'s pro-choice stance (with the above limitations), the nation's second largest Lutheran denomination, the *Lutheran Church - Missouri Synod (LCMS)*, has strongly defended the sanctity of life since the early 1970s. Its resolution 9-07, which was passed at its 1971 synodical convention in Milwaukee, Wisconsin stated, "We affirm that life is God's gift. By reason of the Father's creation and the Son's redemption of man, God has exalted [the human being] above all other creatures and given to him the privilege of becoming His child. Therefore, human life must be treasured, supported, and protected . . . We encourage all people to avoid perverting God's will by resorting to indiscriminate termination of life . . . through such acts as abortion and euthanasia."[175] More recently at its 1998 St. Louis convention, the synod reaffirmed its position on the sanctity of human life in resolution 6-02 stating, "After a quarter of a century abortion continues to be a legal choice in the United States for women who want to terminate an unwanted pregnancy, although the Holy Scriptures clearly teach that this killing of the unborn is an abomination to the Lord (Gen. 9:6, Prov. 6:16–17) . . ."[176]

Because of the split of opinion on the abortion issue between the American Lutheran denominations in the 1970s, an extra-denominational group was needed that could educate all Lutherans on the life issues. In 1974, the *LCMS* held a fundraising dinner to raise seed money for such an organization. The dinner was organized by Jean Garton, the wife of a *LCMS* pastor, and Ralph Bohlmann, the executive director of the *LCMS* Commission on Theology and Church Relations. The dinner was hosted by Dr. Jack Preus, who was then president of that denomination.[177]

After preliminary work to identify volunteers and raise funds, *Lutherans For Life (LFL)* was organized in 1976 through the efforts of

---

174. "Social Statement on Abortion," in Evangelical Lutheran Church of America website. (Chicago, IL, 2007 [cited 21 June 2007]); available from http://www.elca.org/SocialStatements/abortion; INTERNET.

175. "Resolutions on the Sanctity of Human Life by Pro-Life Lutheran Bodies," in Lutherans for Life website. (Nevada, IA, 2007 [cited 11 June 2007]); available from lutheransforlife.org/PDF_Files/Resolutions_-_Lutheran_Church_Bodies.pdf; INTERNET.

176. Ibid.

177. Jean Garton, e-mail interview with the author, November 10, 2007.

Rev. Dr. C. Jack Eichhorst, now the interim pastor of Peace Lutheran Church (ELCA) in Bismarck, North Dakota. In that year, Eichhorst met with Jean Garton, Leigh Jordahl (later Professor of Religion and Classics at the ELCA's Luther College in Decorah, Iowa), Sam Nafzger (now LCMS Executive Director of the Commission on Theology and Church Relations), Michael Rogness (later a professor of homiletics at the ELCA Luther Seminary in St. Paul, Minnesota), Richard John Neuhaus (as mentioned above, now a Roman Catholic priest and editor of the journal *First Things*), and Robert Jensen (later a professor at the ELCA seminary in Gettysburg, Pennsylvania), to create a pan-Lutheran organization which would be devoted to life issues.[178] After two years of discussions and planning, a meeting was held on August 22, 1978 at Concordia College, St. Paul, Minnesota, which officially incorporated *Lutherans For Life*. Jean Garton became the organization's first president, with Dr. Eichhorst elected Vice President, Leigh Jordahl elected Secretary, and Professor Eugene Linse, chairman of the Concordia University-St. Paul department of Political Science, chosen as the organization's first executive director.[179] Dr. Linse began the work of *LFL* by enlisting students at Concordia-St. Paul to volunteer as staff members.[180]

Dr. Jean Garton's tenure as president of *Lutherans For Life* proved to be one of the most visible Protestant pro-life witnesses of the 1970s and 1980s. In organizing the new organization, Dr. Garton sought to enlist women to be the presidents of the *LFL* state affiliates, in order to show the respect that women had for the sanctity of life.[181] In 1974 and 1976, she testified on behalf of the *LCMS* before committees on Capitol Hill to urge passage of the Human Life Amendment.[182] Her statements before Congress marked the first time that a Protestant denomination had publicly advocated for the protection of the unborn after the *Roe* decision.[183]

---

178. "A Brief History of Lutherans for Life," in Lutherans for Life website. (Nevada, IA, 2007 [cited 11 June 2007]); available from http://www.lutheransforlife.org/Who_Are_We/brief_history.htm; INTERNET.

179. Ibid.

180. Jean Garton, e-mail interview with the author, November 10, 2007.

181. Ibid.

182. Ibid.

183. Ibid.

Garton also gained notoriety educating the public about the abortion issue on her pro-life radio program, *Speaking of Life*.[184] She also wrote the highly influential pro-life book *Who Broke the Baby? (1979 and updated in 1998)*, which became a bestseller and was later translated into both Spanish and German and was also converted to video.[185] Garton attributes the book's popularity to its use of simple and non-technical language, and its ability to deconstruct and refute the often misleading pro-choice arguments.[186] She got the idea for the title of the book while preparing a presentation for a pro-life talk. While reviewing her presentation slides, her three-year-old son unexpectedly walked into the room when a slide of an aborted unborn child was being displayed. He quickly asked, "Who broke the baby?"[187] His response to the photo convinced Garton that our adult population was sorely misinformed about the abortion question. In fact, Americans were so misled by pro-choice rhetoric that they couldn't even accept the facts that were patently obvious to a toddler.[188]

In the *Who Broke the Baby?* Garton questions and debunks the abortion slogans that so many people simply take for granted. For instance, in dissecting the pro-choice slogan "Every Child A Wanted Child," Garton writes,

> The EVERY-CHILD-A-WANTED-CHILD concept reduces a child to an object. We usually want "things"—a vacation, a raise, a new car, or a dress. Thus to "want" or to "not want" children is to "thing-ify" them. In our consumer-oriented society, we have created an economic system with no room for children. We do not need them for production on the family farm or for old-age insurance. Rather, they have become a costly luxury that, for some men and women, must provide at least as much satisfaction and gratification as any other object of the "good" life—the sports utility vehicle, the laptop computer, the time-share at a ski resort. The result is that preborn children are caught in the crunch of competing with objects that mark the classic American success syndrome.[189]

184. "A Brief History of Lutherans for Life."

185. Jean Garton, e-mail interview with the author, November 11, 2007.

186. Ibid.

187. Jean Garton, *Who Broke the Baby? What The Abortion Slogans Really Mean.* (Minneapolis, MN: Bethany House, 1998), 7.

188. Ibid., 7.

189. Ibid., 28.

Today, the *Lutherans For Life* national organization is located in Nevada, Iowa, under the direction of its president, Diane Schroeder and its executive director Rev. Dr. James Lamb. Lamb became interested in full-time pro-life ministry after reading the Bible for a year with what he calls "for life eyes."[190] After that year, he became convinced that the life issues, such as abortion, euthanasia, and physician-assisted suicide, were spiritual pitfalls that God, in his Holy Word, has taught us to reject.[191] During his eleven-year tenure, Dr. Lamb has continuously preached the gospel of life at local churches, district churchworker conferences, and with every graduating class of *LCMS* seminarians.[192] He also served as the general editor of the *God's Word For Life* Bible, a pro-life Bible which includes articles by noted Lutheran scholars on each of the life issues.[193] Along with its 15 state federations and over 100 local chapters, *Lutherans For Life* has sought to "witness to the sanctity of human life through education based on the Word of God."[194]

METHODISTS

The *United Methodist Church* (*UMC*), in its 1968 General Convention, first relaxed its position on abortion by stating, "Recognizing that there are certain circumstances under which abortion may be justified from a Christian standpoint, we recommend a study of existing abortion laws."[195] And in doing so, the *UMC* began to move away from the doctrine of its founder, John Wesley, much as the *ELCA* Lutherans had parted ways from the teachings of their founder, Martin Luther. The clear pro-life teachings of both these Protestant leaders have already been shown in chapter 5.

This new pro-choice position was further explained at its 1970 convention, when the denomination asked that the government "remove the regulation of abortion from the criminal code, placing it instead under regulations relating to other procedures of standard medical practice.

190. James Lamb, e-mail interview with the author, September 19, 2007.

191. Ibid.

192. Ibid.

193. Ibid.

194. "A Brief History of Lutherans for Life."

195. "News Archives: Abortion," in the United Methodist Church website. (Nashville, TN, June 1, 2001 [cited 26 June 2007]); available from http://archives.umc.org/umns/backgrounders.asp?ptid=2&story={FB3D4877-CA2B-4BBE-B0A6-B74DAB578C6F}&mid=905; INTERNET.

Abortion would be available only upon request of the person most directly concerned."[196] In this case, it must be assumed that the *UMC* considered the "person most directly concerned" to be the mother, and not the unborn child. The *UMC's* 1972 resolution on abortion allowed "women to be free to make their own responsible decisions concerning the personal and moral questions surrounding the issue of abortion."[197] This was an abrupt change from previous resolutions which recommended that abortion be conducted only in the cases of rape, incest, or another rare occurrence, and only after a review by a panel of physicians.[198]

After the *Roe v. Wade* decision in 1973, the *United Methodist Church* adopted an omnibus resolution on "Health, Welfare and Human Development." In that resolution it stated, "When, through contraceptive or human failure, an unacceptable pregnancy occurs, we believe that a profound regard for unborn human life must be weighed alongside an equally profound regard for fully developed personhood, particularly when the physical, mental, and emotional health of the pregnant woman and her family show reason to be seriously threatened by the new life just forming."[199] Again one is struck by the wording of these resolutions. The quote above references an "unacceptable pregnancy," but it does not explain to whom it was unacceptable, and we must again make assumptions: this time assuming that it was unacceptable to the parents and not to God.

The same resolution also stated that, "We support the legal right to abortion as established by the 1973 Supreme Court [*Roe v. Wade*] decision."[200] As an interesting footnote, the author of that decision, Justice Harry Blackmun, was a practicing member of the *United Methodist Church.*[201]

But the *UMC* did not limit its activism to making changes to its denominational statements. On the contrary, many of its members and clergy were at the forefront of the pro-choice movement. During the years

---

196. "News Archives: Abortion."

197. Joretta Purdue, "United Methodists agreed more on abortion issue 25 years ago," (Washington, D.C., United Methodist News Service (Release #35) (10-21-71B)562, January 21, 1998 [cited 26 June 2007]); available from http://dev.umns.umc.org/98/jan/35.htm; INTERNET.

198. Ibid.

199. "News Archives: Abortion."

200. Ibid.

201. Purdue.

before *Roe v. Wade,* many Methodist clergy were active members of the aforementioned *Clergy Consultation Service,* which referred women to illegal abortion doctors.[202] Methodist Judith McWhorter Widdicombe was also very active in the pro-choice movement, co-founding the *National Abortion Federation,* and also serving as a member of the Board of Directors of the *National Abortion Rights Action League (NARAL).*[203] The *UMC* even allowed *RCRC* to house its headquarters in the Methodist building in Washington, D.C. And this arrangement lasted until 1993, when *RCRC* decided to move into its own offices.[204]

In 1998, the denomination provided some limitations on abortion, stating that "we cannot affirm abortion as an acceptable means of birth control, and we unconditionally reject it as a means of gender selection."[205] In addition, in its current position statement which was written in the year 2000 and can be found in the *United Methodist Church*'s 2004 *Book of Discipline,* states, "Our belief in the sanctity of unborn human life makes us reluctant to approve abortion,"[206] and "we oppose the use of late-term abortion known as dilation and extraction (partial-birth abortion) and call for the end of this practice except when the physical life of the mother is in danger and no other medical procedure is available, or in the case of severe fetal anomalies incompatible with life."[207]

Although the *United Methodist Church* has taken a solidly pro-choice position (with the limitations shown above), it still boasts a number of very vocal pro-life voices. One of the strongest statements by Methodist clergy on the sanctity of human life was the 1992 *Durham Declaration,* which was organized by Rev. Paul Stallsworth, president of the *Taskforce of United Methodists on Abortion and Sexuality (TUMAS),* and was signed by numerous other notable Methodists, including Duke University theology professor Stanley Hauerwas. It states,

> We pledge with God's help to teach our churches that the unborn child is created in the image of God and is one for whom the Son of God died. This child is God's child. This child is part of God's

202. Purdue.

203. Ibid.

204. Ibid.

205. "News Archives: Abortion."

206. Ibid.

207. Ibid.

world. So the life of this child is not ours to take. Therefore, it is sin to take this child's life for reasons whether of birth control, gender selection, convenience, or avoidance of embarrassment . . . We pledge, as people of a community whose sins are forgiven by God, to offer the hope of God's mercy and forgiveness to the woman who has obtained an elective abortion. God's forgiveness and healing are also to be offered to those who have assisted a woman in aborting and now repent. We pledge with God's help, to become a church that hospitably provides safe refuge for the so-called 'unwanted child' and mother. We joyfully welcome and generously support—with prayer, friendship, and material resources—both child and mother. This support includes strong encouragement for the biological father to be a father, in deed, to his child.[208]

This nurturing attitude was also beautifully expressed in Stanley Hauerwas's 1993 article "Abortion Theologically Understood." He writes, "abortion is not about the law, but about what kind of people we are to be as the Church and as Christians."[209] He adds, "The issue is how we as a Christian community can live in positive affirmation of the kind of hospitality that will be a witness to the society that we live in."[210] Hauerwas also touches on the Christian responsibility to welcome all unborn children, even those who are severely ill or disabled, into the world. He writes, "The crucial issue for us as Christians is what kind of people we need to be—capable of welcoming into this world children, some of whom may be born with disabilities and even die."[211]

Another pro-life Methodist is the Rev. William H. Willimon, former dean of the Duke University chapel and professor of Christian Ministry at Duke Divinity School, and currently the Bishop of the North Alabama Conference of *UMC*. Willimon has written about how the pro-choice message alienates those who have experienced an abortion. He writes,

Too many of those who have had abortions feel lonely, guilty, and alienated, in great part because they have been told by an unfaithful church that abortion is 'a private issue,' 'a personal choice.' Therefore, if they are in pain and heartache after abortion, it

208. Paul T. Stallsworth, ed., *The Church and Abortion*. (Nashville: Abingdon Press, 1993), 14.

209. Stanley Hauerwas, "Abortion Theologically Understood," in *The Church and Abortion*, ed. by Paul T. Stallsworth (Nashville: Abingdon Press, 1993), 48.

210. Ibid., 58.

211. Ibid., 61.

becomes a terribly lonely pain. Having told them that their abortion was a private, personal matter, we render their pain private and personal as well, something to be borne alone. This is sub-Christian. In the church, we invite people's pain to go public, to be brought to church and shared with others. This is where true healing begins.[212]

Another thoughtful pro-life voice within Methodism is Richard B. Hays, the George Washington Ivey professor of New Testament at Duke Divinity School. In his book, *The Moral Vision of the New Testament*, Hays points out that abortion is simply not a part of the biblical worldview. He writes, "Thus, to understand ourselves and God in terms of the Bible's story is to know that we are God's creatures. We neither create ourselves nor belong to ourselves. Within this worldview, abortion—whether it be "murder" or not—is wrong for the same reason that murder and suicide are wrong: it presumptuously assumes authority to dispose of life that does not belong to us."[213]

The *UMC* lacked a unified pro-life presence until the 1980s, when Rev. Ken Unger formed the organization *Protestants Protesting Abortion* and led a group of Methodists to the *March for Life,* a peaceful anti-abortion protest held annually in Washington, D.C. Despite this early effort, a more educationally-oriented organization was needed, and in August of 1987, nine United Methodist clerics and lay people formed the aforementioned *Taskforce of United Methodists on Abortion and Sexuality (TUMAS)* in Washington, D.C.[214] Its mission statement states,

> Out of obedience to Jesus Christ, the Taskforce of United Methodists on Abortion and Sexuality works to create—in church and society—esteem for human life at its most vulnerable, specifically for the unborn child and for the woman who contemplates abortion. Therefore, *TUMAS*'s goal is to win the hearts and minds of United Methodists, and to engage in abortion-prevention through theological, pastoral, and social emphases that support human life.[215]

212. William H. Willimon, "The Ministry of Hospitality," in *The Church and Abortion.* ed. by Paul T. Stallsworth (Nashville: Abingdon Press, 1993), 21.

213. Richard B. Hayes, *The Moral Vision of the New Testament: Community, Cross, New Creation.* (San Francisco: Harper Collins Publishers, 1996), 450.

214. "Origin and History of LIFEWATCH," in the Lifewatch website. (Cottleville, MO [cited 26 June 2007]); available from http://lifewatch.org/origin_and_history_of_lifewatch.html; INTERNET.

215. Ibid.

Today, *TUMAS* is actively engaged in educating the Methodist community on the biblical and Wesleyan basis of the sanctity of life, and it also lobbies for pro-life amendments at *UMC* general conventions.[216] *TUMAS* also prints a quarterly newsletter called *Lifewatch*, which is edited by its president, the Rev. Paul Stallsworth. Because of the success of the newsletter, the organization has been commonly referred to by the name *Lifewatch*, as well as *TUMAS*.[217]

While the rights of the unborn have only been defended by a minority of *UMC* clergy, this is not the case in two of the smaller Methodist denominations. For instance, the *Church of the Nazarene* in its Manual of 2005 strongly opposed abortion. It prohibited "induced abortion by any means, when used for either personal convenience or population control,"[218] and it also "oppose[d] laws that allow abortion."[219] And the *Church of the Nazarene* also stated that abortions intended to protect the life of the mother could only be allowed after "sound medical and Christian counseling."[220] Another Methodist denomination, the *Wesleyan Church*, also took a consistent pro-life stand after *Roe v. Wade*. Its 2004 *Book of Discipline* opposed abortion in almost every instance, and it only allowed abortions which were needed to save the life of the mother. Even these abortions required "medical and spiritual counseling" and "very prayerful consideration."[221]

NON-DENOMINATIONAL CHRISTIAN ORGANIZATIONS

Some of the most outspoken support for the sanctity of life within Christianity has come from non-denominational organizations. For instance, the highly influential *National Association of Evangelicals* "passed a 1973 resolution deploring *Roe* 'in strongest possible terms' and declare[ed] that unborn life like all other human life, was a sacred gift from God."[222] In addition, the popular magazine *Christianity Today*, has

216. "Origin and History of LIFEWATCH."

217. Ibid.

218. *Manual of the Church of the Nazarene 2005–2009.* (Kansas City, MO: Nazarene Publishing House, 2005), 53–54.

219. Ibid., 53–54.

220. Ibid., 53–54.

221. *The Discipline of the Wesleyan Church 2004.* (Indianapolis, IN: Wesleyan Publishing House, 2005), 42.

222. Gorney, 339.

published numerous articles since the 1970s imploring Protestants to take up the pro-life cause.[223]

One Christian group that has changed the complexion of the abortion debate is *Concerned Women for America (CWA)*. *CWA* reversed the false perception in the 1960s and 1970s that nearly all American women were in favor of legalized abortion. It also helped balance the media coverage which had been heavily influenced by organizations like the *National Organization for Women (NOW)* and the *National Abortion Rights Action League*, now called *NARAL Pro-Choice America*. Through *CWA's* work, the views of millions of pro-life American women were revealed to the public, and are now regularly reported in the media.

CWA's founder Beverly LeHaye, the wife of *Left Behind* author Tim LeHaye, started the organization after seeing a 1978 television interview with *NOW* founder Betty Friedan.[224] After watching the interview, LeHaye was deeply troubled that Friedan's radical perspectives on religion, family, and human life expressed in the interview were being represented as those of the typical American woman. To combat this perceived misinformation, she started *CWA* the following year.[225]

> "My Dad would look at me with tears running down his face and say, 'I would never cast one vote for a politician that would kill even one of those innocent babies.' He forced me to think about the issue, and the Lord began to convict me. And regardless of how I tried to control it, whenever I spoke on that subject, I couldn't fight the tears."
>
> –Dr. James Dobson

Since that time, *CWA* has defended the sanctity of life in its educational efforts, on Capitol Hill, and for many years on its daily radio program *Beverly LeHaye Live*.[226] The organization has also produced pro-life videos for use in crisis pregnancy centers such as *Hidden Truth: What*

223. Gorney, 340.

224. "History of Concerned Women for America" from the Concerned Woman for America website (Washington, D.C. [cited 7 January 2008]); available from http://www.cwfa.org/history.asp; INTERNET.

225. Ibid.

226. Ibid.

You Deserve to Know About Abortion and *After the Choice.*[227] In 1993, CWA delivered 350,000 petitions to U.S. Senators to urge them to oppose the *Freedom of Choice Act*, a bill which attempted to put the *Roe v. Wade* decision into law.[228]

CWA also lobbied successfully for the passage of the *Partial-Birth Abortion Ban Act* in 1997, and the *Born Alive Infants Protection Act* in 2002.[229] This latter bill made it a federal offense to deny medical treatment to a child who had been born alive during a late-term abortion. The practice of post-abortion abandonment was brought to the attention of the press by Jill Stanek, a nurse at Christ Hospital, a Lutheran medical facility in Oak Lawn, Illinois. Stanek was grieved to find a living aborted child who had been left to die in a dirty linen closet at the hospital. The child later died. Stanek became an activist with *CWA*, and actively lobbied for passage of the bill.[230]

The founder of the popular non-denominational Christian radio program *Focus on the Family*, Dr. James Dobson, has also been outspokenly pro-life.[231] Of all the voices in Christian media, Dobson has probably best explained the pro-life position in terms of the responsibility to love these most defenseless members of our society. In an e-mail interview conducted for this book, Dobson shared how he became convicted about the importance and urgency of the abortion issue. He writes,

> I was working on my Ph.D. at the University of Southern California in the 1960s when cultural opposition to abortion began to erode. Although it wasn't yet legal, many of my professors were supporting abortion. I hadn't thought through some of the implications of the issue yet, and I was beginning to buy into the notion that abortion was OK.
>
> Then I would go home and have dinner with my folks. And I would tell my dad, "You know, Dad, there are these kids; they're born in the inner city. Nobody wants them. They come into the world and there's nobody to take care of them. And they are often abused or left on the street . . . " And my Dad would look at me with tears running down his face and say, "I would never cast one vote for a politician that would kill even one of those innocent

227. "History of Concerned Women for America."
228. Ibid.
229. Ibid.
230. Ibid.
231. Risen and Thomas, 295.

babies." He forced me to think about the issue, and the Lord began to convict me. And regardless of how I tried to control it, whenever I spoke on that subject, I couldn't fight the tears.

By the time the Supreme Court legalized abortion in 1973, I was firmly against it on moral and scriptural grounds. In 1990, when I pledged [at the *Rally for Life in* Washington, D.C.] never to cast a vote for a politician who would take the life of an innocent baby, I was quoting my father, who had long since passed away. Focus on the Family's pro-life commitment is ultimately the result of my Dad's godly influence.[232]

Dobson's conviction was put into action in support of pregnancy care centers across the nation, and today *Focus on the Family* produces much of the literature and audio-visual resources that are used to counsel women at these centers.[233] To further educate women who are contemplating abortion, *Focus on the Family* started its *Option Ultrasound Project*, which has allowed many pregnancy centers to become medical clinics where women can see, through the use of ultrasounds, the child growing within them.[234] Dobson has estimated that over 72,000 babies have been saved from abortion through this program alone.[235]

Dobson's consistent witness on the abortion question can also be seen in his 1994 work, *Children at Risk*, which he wrote with former *Family Research Council* head, Gary Bauer. In the book, Dobson reflects on today's generation of newborns. These children will live in a world where abortion is commonplace, and will probably be taught that the taking of life in the womb is ethical. He describes meeting a young boy named Josh and shares his reflections on the meeting,

> I thought about the 25 million little babies who have been killed through abortion since the Supreme Court legalized their slaughter in 1973. Their numbers would amount to ten percent of today's entire population of Americans . . . Not only do I mourn for those millions of babies who were taken from their places of safety, but I also worry about Josh and his contemporaries who *were* permitted to live. Theirs will not be an easy journey, either. The same twisted

---

232. James Dobson, e-mail interview with the author, November 29, 2007.

233. Ibid.

234. Ibid.

235. Ibid.

philosophy that permits us to kill infants with impunity is now prevalent throughout the Western world.[236]

Another influential pro-life Christian group is the non-denominational *Faith and Action* headed by the Rev. Rob Schenck. Schenck and his twin brother Paul are both converts from Judaism and are probably best known for their roles as defendants in a number of court cases which dealt with the legality of federal injunctions against abortion clinic demonstrators. These cases culminated in a victory at the U.S. Supreme Court in the case *Schenck v. Pro-Choice Network* (1997). It was that case which unanimously decided that a "floating buffer zone," which was an injunction to keep protesters a certain distance away from abortion clinic clients and employees, was a violation of the First Amendment of the Constitution.[237] The court did allow a "fixed buffer zone," however, which could keep protesters a certain distance from abortion facilities.[238] Schenck is also the author of the book *Ten Words That Will Change a Nation*. This work explains the importance of posting the Ten Commandments in public buildings, and it also speaks out strongly in defense of unborn life.

In 1992, Rev. Schenck and his brother Paul (who was then a pastor at Hope Church in Buffalo, New York) came up with the idea of starting a Christian ministry which would ac-tively engage the federal government and urge it to uphold biblical moral-ity.[239] After two years of prayerful consideration, the brothers moved to the Washington, D.C. area. Upon arriving, they noticed that the need

> "Mr. President, God will hold you to account for the babies."
>
> –Rev. Rob Schenck

for biblical witness was especially acute at the U.S. Supreme Court: an in-stitution where the pro-life perspective was sorely underrepresented and pro-choice legal institutions like the *American Civil Liberties Union (ACLU)* were well-entrenched.[240] Today, *Faith and Action's* offices are located just

---

236. Jacoby, 98.

237. "Schenck et al. *v.* Pro-Choice Network of Western New York et al." from the Cornell University Law School website (Ithaca, NY [cited 7 January 2008]); available from http://www.law.cornell.edu/supct/html/95-1065.ZS.html; INTERNET.

238. Ibid.

239. Rob Schenck, telephone interview with the author, January 3, 2008.

240. Ibid.

across the street from the Supreme Court building, and it is there that organization works to be a Christian presence to the court's justices and staff.

Rev. Schenck is also known for some of the courageous stands he has taken on behalf of the preborn, whether in front of abortion clinics or within the public square. An example of one of those stands occurred on Christmas Eve, 1996.[241] Having been invited to a Christmas Eve service at the Washington National Cathedral, Schenck noticed, upon arrival, that President Clinton, Mrs. Clinton, and daughter Chelsea were also present. Schenck had been deeply troubled by Clinton's April 1996 veto of the partial-birth abortion ban which had been overwhelmingly passed by Congress the previous year, and he felt that it was his responsibility as a clergy member to admonish the President for allowing this gruesome procedure to continue. Finding the opportunity to approach the President while standing in line for communion, Schenck told him, "Mr. President, God will hold you to account for the babies."[242] This short statement cost Schenck a few hours of interrogation by the Secret Service after the service,[243] but it showed the type of mettle that has been characteristic of his entire career.

In 1996, *Faith and Action* started the *National Memorial for the Pre-Born*, a non-denominational worship service held every year on the anniversary of the *Roe v. Wade* decision—January 22. Since that time, the Schencks have usually held the worship service inside one of the U.S. Senate office buildings. And in doing so, they have created a unique pro-life presence within Congress itself.[244]

Faith and Action also has a sister ministry, the *National Clergy Council (NCC)*, which educates the clergy on the many ethical issues which confront Christians today, including abortion. It boasts a membership of over three thousand evangelical pastors, and it holds regular leadership conferences in various cities across the country.[245]

---

241. "Abortion Foe Speaks to Clinton," *St. Paul Pioneer Press (MN)*, December 27, 1996, 4A.

242. Schenck.

243. Ibid.

244. Ibid.

245. Ibid.

ORTHODOX CHRISTIANS

In his book *The Sacred Gift of Life: Orthodox Christianity and Bioethics*, the Very Rev. John Breck, former professor of New Testament and Ethics at St. Vladimir's Orthodox Theological Seminary states, "The Orthodox stance on the issue of abortion has never been in doubt. From biblical times to the present, abortion has been regarded as the morally condemnable act of destroying an innocent life."[246] He adds, "Traditionally, the only grounds on which the Church can accept abortion are . . . true and serious threats to a mother's life."[247]

Interestingly, this high valuation of human life has been attributed to the Orthodox emphasis on *theosis*. Breck writes, "Every man and woman is created according to God's own 'image' and 'likeness' (Gen. 1:26–27). Everyone, without exception, possesses the capacity for virtue, holiness, and ultimately *theosis* or 'deification': a full and eternal participation in the divine energies or attributes. That is why [the Orthodox] Christian tradition stresses so emphatically that human life is sacred."[248]

The Orthodox Christian faith has been blessed with not only a tradition of pro-life doctrine, but also with strong pro-life organizations. One such group of pro-life Orthodox Christians is *Orthodox Christians for Life (OCLife)*. OCLife was started in 1986 by Rev. Edward Pehanich (an Orthodox priest), John Protopapas (now a deacon in the Orthodox Church), and his wife Valerie Protopapas.[249] It currently has over 800 members and five chapters nationwide, and works primarily to educate the Orthodox Christian church on the sanctity of human life.[250] OCLife also produces a quarterly journal, *Rachel's Children*, and leads an annual delegation of hundreds of Eastern Orthodox Christians in the *March for Life*.[251] In the years 1989 and 1990, the marchers were led by four U.S. Orthodox bishops.[252]

---

246. John Breck, *The Sacred Gift of Life: Orthodox Christianity and Bioethics*. (Crestwood, NY: St. Vladimir's Press. 1998), 148.

247. Ibid., 248.

248. Ibid., 19.

249. John Protopapas, e-mail interview by the author, August 12, 2007.

250. Ibid.

251. Ibid.

252. Ibid.

In the year 2000, another Orthodox pro-life organization, *Alpha Omega Life*, was begun by Vera Faith Lord with the blessing of His Eminence Metropolitan Maximos of Pittsburgh.[253] Ms. Lord has been a courageous witness for the unborn, sharing her own experience with abortion and the healing that is available through Jesus Christ at countless Orthodox churches.[254] Her personal witness of the tragedy of abortion has created a new awareness of God's plan for human life within the Orthodox community, and has also highlighted the importance of offering reconciliation to post-abortive men and women.[255]

PENTECOSTALS

Since the *Roe v. Wade* decision, the Pentecostal denominations have, on the whole, remained steadfast in their defense of life in the womb. The largest U.S. Pentecostal denomination, the *Assemblies of God*, states that, "The Assemblies of God is unashamedly pro-life. Even though a United States Supreme Court decision legalized abortion in 1973, abortion is still immoral and sinful. This stand is founded on the biblical truth that all human life is created in the image of God (Genesis 1:27). From that truth issues the long-standing Christian view that aborting the life of a developing child is evil."[256]

Probably one of the best known Pentecostal religious leaders in the United States is the televangelist Pat Robertson. Although ordained as a Southern Baptist pastor, Robertson has espoused many of spirit-filled beliefs of charismatic and Pentecostals Christians. He has also been unapologetically pro-life, with abortion being a common topic on his *The 700 Club* television program.[257] Robertson has also leveraged his television fame to work for change within the political arena. For instance, he made the sanctity of life a major plank in his 1988 Presidential campaign. Robertson also created the *Christian Coalition*, which has been highly effective in bringing the abortion issue into the national consciousness.

---

253. Vera Faith Lord, e-mail interview by the author, July 30, 2007.

254. Ibid.

255. Ibid.

256. "Beliefs: Abortion," from the Assemblies of God website. (Springfield, MO, 1985 [cited 3 July 2007]); available from http://ag.org/top/Beliefs/contempissues_01_abortion .cfm; INTERNET.

257. Risen and Thomas, 187.

The *Christian Coalition* has also been a powerful political force within the Republican Party, and in its heyday in the 1980s it boasted over 400,000 members.[258]

PRESBYTERIANS

In 1970, The Presbyterian Church in the United States of America (PCUS), and the United Presbyterian Church in the United States of America (UPCUSA), both passed similar statements at their conventions liberalizing their views on abortion. The PCUS stated,

> The willful termination of pregnancy by medical means on the considered decision of a pregnant woman may on occasion be morally justifiable. Possible justifying circumstances would include medical indications of physical or mental deformity, conception as a result of rape or incest, conditions under which the physical or mental health of either mother or child would be gravely threatened, or the socio-economic condition of the family," and that "Medical intervention should be made available to all who desire and qualify for it, not just to those who can afford preferential treatment.[259]

The UPCUSA shared these sentiments in its own proclamation on abortion,

> the artificial or inducted termination of pregnancy is a matter of the careful ethical decision of the patient, her physician, and her pastor or other counselor and therefore should not be restricted by law, except that it be performed under the direction and control of a properly licensed physician . . . urges the establishment of medically sound, easily available, and low-cost abortion services; the support and expansion of responsible counseling services on problem pregnancies; and the support for groups working responsibly for repeal of abortion laws which are not in harmony [with this position] . . .[260]

---

258. J. Christopher Soper, *Evangelical Christianity in the United States and Great Britain.* (New York: New York University Press, 1994), 107.

259. *Presbyterian Social Witness Policy Compilation.* (Louisville, KY: Advisory Committee on Social Witness Policy of the General Assembly Council, Presbyterian Church (U.S.A.), 2000), 427.

260. Ibid., 427.

These two statements marked the beginning of the Presbyterian Church's abandonment of its traditional doctrine on the sinfulness of abortion. Like the mainline Lutheran and Methodist denominations which also departed from the ethical doctrines taught by their Reformation leaders, in 1970 the Presbyterian Church reversed the opinion of its historical founder, John Calvin (see chapter 5).

In the 1980s, the Presbyterian denominations became extensively involved in pro-choice activism. In 1982, the *PCUS*, reaffirmed its membership in *RCAR*, the earlier title for *RCRC*, and also provided its Mission Board with guidance on efforts to promote "reproductive freedom."[261] In 1983, the *PCUS* and the *UPCUSA* merged, forming what we now know as the *Presbyterian Church of the United States of America (PCUSA)*. The new denomination's 1983 statement on abortion, was, according to former *Presbyterians Pro-Life* president, Rev. Ben Sheldon, "the most radical position of any U.S. denomination."[262]

Included in the statement was the following assertion, "The decision to terminate pregnancy may be an affirmation of one's covenant responsibility to accept the limits of human resources. Because we understand the morality of abortion to be a question of stewardship for life, the responsible decision to choose abortion may arise from analysis of the projected resources for caregiving in a specific situation."[263] And although the statement later urges the "care of unwed mothers,"[264] it fails to explain how abortion can be avoided when congregations offer assistance to needy women. Instead, it circumvents the congregation's responsibility altogether by offering abortion as an ethical means of avoiding monetary difficulties.

Other portions of the 1983 statement make little theological sense at all. One section states, "Biblical faith emphasizes the need for personal moral choice and holds that persons stand ultimately accountable to God for their moral choices. The freedom to do what one judges most appropriate in an abortion decision is qualified by the fact that the purpose of such decision is the responsible exercise of stewardship." After the reading the statement above, one is struck by the *PCUSA*'s boldfaced attempt

---

261. *Presbyterian Social Witness Policy Compilation*, 427.

262. Ben Sheldon, telephone interview by author, August 24, 2007.

263. *Presbyterian Social Witness Policy Compilation*, 429.

264. Ibid., 429.

to shoehorn a "pro-choice" slogan into the biblical message. Somehow, the Christian's "responsible exercise of stewardship" has trumped his obligation to obey God's holy law. And in its zeal to protect the availability of abortion, the *PCUSA* has forgotten that obedience to God's commandments must take precedence over one's "need for personal moral choice."

In its conclusion, the statement affirms existing laws which protect abortion rights.[265] It also calls on the government to fund abortions for those who could not afford them.[266] According to Rev. Sheldon, it is the radical nature of this 1983 statement which helped boost the active membership of *Presbyterians Pro-Life.*[267]

In its 1992 policy statement on abortion, the *PCUSA* explained that pro-choice activism was an integral component of its social justice ministry. The statement's section entitled "The Church and the Law," has also been effectively used to defend the *PCUSA*'s membership in *RCRC*. It states,

> . . . We believe that in the shaping of the future law, the following affirmations are of vital consideration. a. The state has a limited legitimate interest in regulating abortions and in restricting abortions in certain circumstances. b. Within this context of the state's limited legitimate interest, no law should impose criminal penalties against any women who chooses or physician who performs a medically safe abortion. c. Within this same context of the state's limited legitimate interest, no law should deny access to safe and affordable services for the persons seeking to terminate a problem pregnancy. d. No law or administrative decision should provide for a complete ban on abortion. e. No law or administrative decision should (1) limit access to abortions; (2) limit information and counseling concerning abortions; or (3) limit or prohibit public funding for necessary abortions for the socially and economically disadvantaged. f. No law should prohibit access to, nor the practice of, contraceptive measures. g. No law should sanction any action intended to harm or harass those persons contemplating or deciding to have an abortion. h. No law should condone mandatory or forced abortion or sterilization. Such laws should be abolished where they do exist.[268]

265. *Presbyterian Social Witness Policy Compilation*, 429–30.

266. Ibid., 429–30.

267. Sheldon.

268. *Presbyterian Social Witness Policy Compilation*, 436–37.

Despite the denomination's consistent pro-choice stand, it has proposed some limits to the practice of abortion. For instance in 1997, the denomination provided a warning against the gruesome practice of partial-birth abortion. It wrote, "the 209th General Assembly (1997) of the Presbyterian Church (U.S.A.) offer[s] a word of counsel to the church and our culture that the procedure known as intact dilation and extraction (commonly called "partial-birth" abortion) of a baby who could live outside the womb is of grave moral concern and should be considered only if the mother's physical life is endangered by the pregnancy."[269] At its 2002 convention it also provided a warning against any abortion performed after viability (the time when a child could be expected to survive outside of the womb). That convention stated,

> The ending of a pregnancy after the point of fetal viability is a matter of grave moral concern to us all, and may be undertaken only in the rarest of circumstances and after prayer and/or pastoral care, when necessary to save the life of the woman, to preserve the woman's health in circumstances of a serious risk to the woman's health, to avoid fetal suffering as a result of untreatable life-threatening medical anomalies, or in cases of incest or rape.[270]

The first meeting to organize a pro-life organization within the *PCUSA* occurred at a young ministers' conference at Montreat, North Carolina in October 1976.[271] Three pastors at this conference, Rev. Bruce Davis, Rev. Andrew White, and Rev. Thomas Warren, created the organization *Southern Presbyterians Pro-Life* in the spring of 1978.[272] However, it was not until a meeting at Columbia Seminary in Decatur, Georgia on March 21, 1979, that *Presbyterians Pro-Life (PPL)* was officially established.[273] It was at that meeting that Mrs. Eleanor Blizzard of Columbia, South Carolina was elected the chairman of the organization's board of

269. *Presbyterian Social Witness Policy Compilation*, 436–37.

270. *Presbyterian Social Witness Policy Compilation*. in the Presbyterian Church, USA website. (Louisville, KY: Advisory Committee on Social Witness Policy of the General Assembly Council, Presbyterian Church (U.S.A.), 2007 [cited 29 August 2007]). available from http://index.pcusa.org/NXT/gateway.dll/socialpolicy/chapter00000.htm?fn=default .htm$f=templates$3.0; INTERNET.

271. Marie Bowen, e-mail interview by author, August 8, 2007.

272. Ibid.

273. Ibid.

directors.[274] Since that time, *PPL* has lobbied to reverse the *PCUSA's* pro-choice position statements, and has also worked to educate Presbyterians on the sanctity of human life.[275]

PPL was led by its president, the Rev. William T. Wing, Jr. in the early 1980s, and its president Rev. Ben Sheldon from 1984–1995.[276] In the fall of 1986, Terry Schlossberg was invited to become *PPL's* first full-time paid executive director, and its offices were moved to Burke, Virginia.[277] Under Ms. Schlossberg's tenure, *PPL* organized dozens of additional chapters and expanded the readership of its newsletter, the *PPL News,* to 35,000.[278]

At *PCUSA* conventions during these early years, *PPL* actively lobbied for a study which would reconsider the denomination's pro-choice doctrine. Such a study was actually conducted in 1988, after *PPL* invited Mother Teresa to speak on its behalf at that year's convention.[279] Unfortunately, the study did not substantially change the *PCUSA* position on abortion. In 1992, *PPL* was also active at the *PCUSA* convention in Minneapolis, Minnesota, and it provided input to the statement *Problem Pregnancies and Abortion.* But this document, which attempted to represent all the disparate views in the denomination on the subject, only led to more confusion on the abortion question.[280]

In the 1990s, *PPL* successfully lobbied for the addition of a "Relief of Conscience" option in the *PCUSA's* Medical Benefits Plan. The denomination had previously added abortion services to its health care plan, and many Presbyterian churches became concerned that they might be participating in the funding of abortions. "Relief of Conscience" solved this dilemma by allowing pro-life churches to opt out of having their dues pay for abortions that were covered under the plan.[281] It was also during these years that Ms. Schlossberg, along with Elizabeth Achtemeier, wrote the influential book, *Not My Own.* This book asserts that a right view of

274. Marie Bowen, e-mail interview by author, August 8, 2007.

275. Ibid.

276. Ibid.

277. Ibid.

278. Ibid.

279. Ibid.

280. Ibid.

281. Ibid.

abortion is vital for the church if the Bible is to be correctly preached and the sacraments are to be faithfully administered.[282]

In 2005, Ms. Marie Bowen replaced Ms. Schlossberg as the organization's Executive Director, and its offices were moved to Pittsburgh, Pennsylvania.[283] The following year, *PPL* again won a major victory, passing yet another statement on late-term abortions at that year's *PCUSA* convention. That amendment stated that "the lives of viable unborn babies—those able to survive outside the womb if delivered—ought to be preserved and cared for and not to aborted."[284]

Over the years, *PPL*'s efforts have been directed primarily toward the *PCUSA* since that denomination has been so vocally pro-choice. However, a smaller Presbyterian denomination, the *Presbyterian Church of America (PCA)*, has been active in the defense of the unborn. One of the *PCA*'s most recognizable ministers was the late Dr. D. James Kennedy, who was chancellor of Knox Theological Seminary. Kennedy was also pastor of the over 10,000 member Coral Ridge Presbyterian Church in Ft. Lauderdale, Florida, and he often preached about the sanctity of life from the pulpit, and on his *Coral Ridge Hour* television program.[285] Another seminary of the *PCA*, Covenant Theological Seminary in St. Louis, has also had a history of activism on the abortion issue. Many of its seminarians participated in prayer vigils in front of abortion clinics during the 1980s, and these efforts were actively encouraged by the seminary president at the time, Dr. William Barker.[286]

The Presbyterian Church has also been blessed with individual leaders who have called the Christian community to action. One of the most prominent thinkers on the sanctity of life in the twentieth century was the writer and theologian Francis Schaeffer.[287] Schaeffer was a member of the *Orthodox Presbyterian Church* and he and his wife Edith started the *L'Abri Fellowship*, a Christian ministry, in Switzerland in 1955.[288] Schaeffer also

282. Marie Bowen, e-mail interview by author, August 8, 2007.
283. Ibid.
284. Ibid.
285. Risen and Thomas, 210.
286. Ibid., 142.
287. Ibid., 121.
288. Ibid., 123.

wrote the 1979 pro-life book *Whatever Happened to the Human Race?* with C. Everett Koop (who later became the U.S. Surgeon General).[289]

In the book, he calls on pro-lifers to make a concerted effort to end abortion. He also suggests many ways in which the average Christian might get involved. These include educating society about the abortion epidemic, picketing abortion clinics, promoting the pro-life perspective through the press, working in crisis pregnancy centers, and participating in the political arena.[290] He writes, "But above all, *we must never be silent.* The point is that everyone *can* be involved and it will take all our help to stop this destruction of human lives . . . There is no end to the ways in which we all can work to protect the dignity of every human life."[291] Schaeffer also published the *Christian Manifesto* in 1981, which advocated the use of civil disobedience to end abortion.[292]

R. C. Sproul, the famed Presbyterian preacher and former professor at *Reformed Theological Seminary,* has also been a consistent pro-life witness. Sproul, who is probably best known for his weekly *Renewing Your Mind* radio program, wrote the book, *Abortion: A Rational Look at an Emotional Issue.* Much as Schaeffer had done a decade before, Sproul calls upon all Christians to actively work to end the scourge of abortion. He writes, "The struggle against abortion is difficult, but it is worthy. The longer it lasts, the more babies will be slain. The longer laws allowing abortion-on-demand remain in effect, the more likely it is that society will be hardened in heart. Continuing the struggle against abortion is not enough. We must accelerate our efforts until no human child is destroyed under the sanction of law."[293]

289. Risen and Thomas, 122.

290. C. Everett Koop, MD and Francis A. Schaeffer, *Whatever Happened to the Human Race?* (Westchester, Ill.: Crossway Books, 1979), 136–37.

291. Ibid., 138.

292. Risen and Thomas, 121.

293. R. C. Sproul, *Abortion: A Rational Look at an Emotional Issue.* (Colorado Springs, CO: NavPress, 1990), 156.

8

Headcount

The Percentage of Christianity That Is Pro-Life

After taking a look at the divergent views of all of the Christian denominations shown in the previous chapter, one might hold the mistaken belief that the Christian church really is 50% pro-life and 50% pro-choice. But as Table 1 shows, in the year 2000, and clearly by a large majority (72%), the Christian church was overwhelmingly pro-life.

TABLE 1

	In Billions			In Billions	
	Year 2000	% of total	10 year Growth Rate %	Year 2010	% of total
Total Membership of Christianity	1.971	100.00%		2.245	100.00%
Pro-Life Denominations					
Roman Catholic Church	1.057	53.63%	13.73%	1.202	53.56%
Orthodox Churches	0.215	10.91%	5.58%	0.227	10.11%
Pentecostals	0.100	5.07%	23.10%	0.123	5.48%
US Pro-Life Lutherans	0.003	0.15%	15.41%	0.003	0.15%
US Southern Baptists	0.016	0.81%	15.41%	0.018	0.82%

	Year 2000	% of total	10 year Growth Rate %	Year 2010	% of total
Church of Nigeria Anglican	0.015	0.76%	16.80%	0.018	0.78%
Adventists	0.017	0.86%	15.41%	0.020	0.87%
Total of Pro-Life Denominations	1.423	72.20%		1.611	71.78%
Pro-Choice Denominations					
Presbyterians/ Reformed	0.080	4.06%	15.41%	0.092	4.11%
United Methodists	0.012	0.61%	15.41%	0.014	0.62%
Other Lutherans	0.060	3.04%	15.41%	0.069	3.08%
Other Anglican/Episcopalians	0.065	3.30%	16.80%	0.076	3.38%
Other Pro-Choice Christians (Assumed)	0.331	16.79%	15.41%	0.382	17.02%
Total of Pro-Choice Denominations	0.548	27.80%		0.633	28.22%
Total	1.971			2.245	

Notes:

1) Total Christian population number obtained by taking year 2000 2M Christian total and subtracting 29K JW and LDS membership.

2) All data obtained from *World Christian Encyclopedia* vol.1 2nd ed. ed. By David B. Barrett, George Kurian, and Todd M. Johnson. New York: Oxford University Press, 2001), 4., except for . . .

3) Used Church of Nigeria, Adventist, Southern Baptist, Methodist totals from "Largest Religious Bodies," from the Adherents.com website (18 May 2007 [accessed September 5, 2007]) available from http://www.adherents.com/adh_rb .html#International; INTERNET.

4) Used for Lutheran totals "Number of Lutherans Worldwide Increases to Nearly 64 Million," from the Lutheran World Federation web site Geneva, 24 January 2001 (Lutheran World Information) [accessed September 5, 2007], available from http://www.lutheranworld.org/News/LWI/EN/231.*EN.html*; *INTERNET.*

5) Used for 2000 Presbyterian total "A 'Major Step Forward in Unity' In Reformed Family Of Churches," from World Alliance of Reformed Churches website (Geneva, January 2, 2006 [accessed September 6, 2007]) available from http://warc.jalb .de/warcajsp/side.jsp?news_id=631&part_id=0&navi=6; INTERNET.

6) Used for 2000 Pentecostal total "Pentecostals," from the biblia.com website (April 2006 [accessed September 5, 2007]) available from http://biblia.com/christianity2/3b-pentecostals.htm; INTERNET.

7) Used 1990-2000 growth rates to project 2010 membership numbers from 2000 totals. Protestant denominations without growth rates in the World Christian Encyclopedia were given the generic Protestant growth rate.

The data from this analysis was taken primarily from two sources: *The World Christian Encyclopedia*, and *Adherents.com*. In performing the study, a very conservative technique was utilized which assumed that denominations which were not known to be pro-life were pro-choice. That is, the methodology erred heavily on the pro-choice side by categorizing any denomination which had an *unknown* position on abortion as pro-choice. But even with this methodology, the study still arrived at a very high number (72%) of Christians who worship in pro-life denominations.

Taking into consideration the large number of unaffiliated pro-life churches that exist in the world, it is highly likely that more than 75% of the world's Christian churches are pro-life, or in other words, the Christian church is pro-life by at least a 3 to 1 margin. So the usual media message that gives the impression that the Christian faith is split evenly on the abortion issue is simply not true. In fact, the numbers reveal that Christianity is overwhelmingly pro-life.

The previous data doesn't show whether the lay members of Christian denominations necessarily agree with their church leaders' positions on abortion. Unfortunately, there has not been any systematic worldwide poll of the opinions of the laity on abortion. One would imagine that while there are some pro-choice lay people who are members of pro-life denominations, in a like manner there are undoubtedly some pro-life laypeople who are members of pro-choice denominations. Because of this diversity, the official doctrines of each individual denomination are a more useful determinate of the overall views of Christianity on abortion, since they are often arrived at with more theological and historical deliberation, as well as more denominational consensus, than might be derived from a random opinion sample.

The numerical study shown in Table 1 also projected out to the year 2010 to discover where the opinion within Christianity might be headed, and it appears that pro-life percentages will likely remain constant from the 2000 numbers at 72%. If anything, it is not expected that the Christian church will become more pro-choice over time. Rather, the prediction is that the huge growth of Pentecostalism in world Christianity should result in a higher percentage of pro-life Christians in the decades to come. This change may have already occurred, since some sources have recently estimated the Pentecostal world population to be much higher than has been assumed in the study. For instance, in the November/December 2006 French journal *Le Point,* the population of Pentecostals worldwide was estimated to be between 400-500 million.[1]

This statistical analysis should provide the average pro-life Christian with some additional confidence in the current and future pro-life majority within Christianity. Many pro-life activists who have labored for many years experience burn-out, and they arrive at the false conclusion that no one seems to care about defending innocent human life in the womb. This numerical study shows that this perception is simply not true. In fact, the Christian faith is pro-life by a 3 to 1 margin, and is likely to become even more so in the foreseeable future.

1. "Le Christianisme dans le monde," *Le Point.* Hors-série, no. 11, Novembre-Décembre 2006, 11.

9

Conclusion

An Appeal to Pro-Choice Christians

THIS BOOK CONCLUDES WITH an appeal to pro-choice Christians. The research in this book has revealed that the Bible clearly indicates the sinfulness of abortion, and it has also shown that the church has historically held a consistent moral position in defense of the sanctity of human life. Indeed, Scripture and history have shown that God has *not* been silent on the issue of abortion. On the contrary, He has revealed Himself to be 100% pro-life. *A Love for Life* has also demonstrated that the Christian faith is, even today, overwhelmingly pro-life, by a 3 to 1 margin. This large majority of pro-life witness, will, in all likelihood, remain consistent or even become more pronounced in the future.

But even with the preponderance of the evidence, there will still be many Christians who will remain convinced that there are complicated family situations and desperate hardship cases where abortion remains a justifiable answer to a very difficult situation. Others might be concerned that taking a strong pro-life position might require one to sit in judgment of women who have had abortions. For those individuals, the words of J. W. Rogerson, an emeritus professor of biblical studies at the University of Sheffield, might prove helpful. He writes,

> Can we, at one and the same time, be under the imperative of love, and be satisfied with a society that denies to the unborn the possibility of living? What sort of society is it that leaves to small voluntary agencies [Crisis Pregnancy Centers] to try to persuade mothers who are bearing "unwanted" children to let those children live, while there are many families in which love will make

a full life possible for "unwanted" and "rejected" children? It is in no part of this essay to adopt a superior moral attitude towards mothers who find themselves bearing unwanted children. What a Christian society ought to do, however, is to stress that the love of God stretching out to the unwanted and the unworthy is at the heart of the gospel, and that the practical application of this imperative in all its ramifications is a task laid upon the Church.[1]

Stanley Hauerwas, the Methodist theologian who was referenced earlier in the book, also sheds a great deal of light on abortion and the Christian life, and his quote is worth repeating. He writes, "Abortion is not about the law, but about what kind of people we are to be as the Church and as Christians."[2] He adds, "The issue is how we as a Christian community can live in positive affirmation of the kind of hospitality that will be a witness to the society that we live in."[3]

The words of Rogerson and Hauerwas resonate because they point to the heart of the matter: how Christians respond to those in crisis pregnancies says everything about their walk with Christ. In many Christian churches today, the spirituality of the individual has been stressed to the detriment of life within the Christian community. However, the church should be a place where a woman who finds herself in an unexpected pregnancy can go to receive the support of her fellow Christians. This support should include counseling, spiritual, medical, and financial assistance to get her through this difficult time and give her the support she needs to choose life for her child. The church should also be a place of forgiveness for an out-of-wedlock birth, or for the woman who has experienced an abortion, not a place of "superior moral attitude."

Ultimately, the abortion question comes down to how the body of Christ chooses to live. The Bible says in 1 John 4:11–12, "since God so loved us, we also ought to love one another. No one has ever seen God: but if we love one another, God lives in us and his love is made complete in us." How will Christians live out this moral imperative of love? Will the church "solve" a crisis pregnancy by choosing death for the child, and a life of uncertainty and regret for his or her parents? Or will it redouble its efforts in Christian love to assist each mother to have her baby and raise

---

1. J. W. Rogerson, "Using the Bible in the Debate About Abortion." in *Abortion and the Sanctity of Human Life*, ed. by J. H. Channer (Exeter, UK: Paternoster Ltd., 1985), 89.

2. Hauerwas, "Abortion Theologically Understood," 48.

3. Ibid., 58.

that child to be a beloved child of Jesus? Taking such a stand won't be easy. It will involve personal sacrifice, and even the need to change one's own priorities in order to assist in the rearing of a child. But as any parent knows, the gifts of our time that are given to each precious gift of God are often returned one-hundred fold.

In every crisis pregnancy situation, if the question is asked, "What kind of people are we to be as the church and as Christians?" then the question of whether to advise another person to have an abortion will have already been answered. The Christian must choose life: the choice to love and support another person in need, and in that way follow the gospel of the One who is life.

> *Deuteronomy 30:19 Now choose life, so that you and your children may live and that you may love the Lord your God, listen to his voice, and hold fast to him.*

Appendix I

Current Denominational Statements on Abortion

AFRICAN METHODIST EPISCOPAL CHURCH
Underlined portion of "Consideration of the Abortion Issue," 1977

W E RECOGNIZE THAT GOD created all people with a spirit in His own image for His own purpose. It is this fact that endows each human life with a certain sanctity. The scriptures reveal that this setting-apart for God's work through His "sacrificial love" begins from or even before the womb. Furthermore, they warn us that God forbids the deliberate destruction of such life—at any stage. If we acknowledge and respect the God-given sanctity of human life which begins at conception, then abortion, which represents deliberate destruction of that life created by God, is a violation of that sanctity. Throughout the Old and the New Testament, such an act is forbidden. Thus, in the vast majority of cases, the expediency of abortion-on-demand does not provide an acceptable alternative to the problem pregnancy.

The means of relieving the unwanted child of the burden of an undesirable quality of life, or the unwanting parent of the burden of parenthood at an undesirable time does not lie in the destruction of the new life. Rather, it requires a diligent, active effort, directed by God, to seek first to recognize and prevent the circumstances leading to problem pregnancies. We must also surround each parent and child with love and provide them with concrete spiritual, social, economic and educational assistance.

It remains that there are certain conditions where the problem of a pregnancy is not clearly that of the unwanted child or the unwanting parent. For example, in the situation in which the pregnancy and childbirth clearly jeopardize the life of the mother, abortion is a life-saving measure for the mother.

Under these circumstances, the church must join the parents and family in prayer for guidance by the Spirit so that the Lord's will might be done.[1]

AMERICAN BAPTIST CHURCHES USA

8006.5:12/87 Resolution Concerning Abortion and Ministry in the Local Church

The General Board of American Baptist Churches in the U.S.A. has solicited and received significant response through hearings, letters and questionnaires from individuals and congregations across the country. The response indicates that American Baptists believe that ministry to persons in situations of crisis pregnancy and abortion is a concern that primarily affects the local churches to continue studying these issues, prayerfully seeking, under the guidance of the Holy Spirit, to come to a position that will direct them in ministry. The role of the General Board in this matter is not to speak to churches, but to assist them in carrying out ministry and advocacy according to their convictions. Therefore, as a reflection of American Baptist thought, this resolution is offered to assist our churches.

As American Baptists, members of a covenant community of believers in Jesus Christ, we acknowledge life as a sacred and gracious gift of God. We affirm that God is the Creator of all life, that human beings are created in the image of God, and Christ is Lord of life. Recognizing this gift of life, we find ourselves struggling with the painful and difficult issue of abortion. Genuine diversity of opinion threatens the unity of our fellowship, but the nature of the covenant demands mutual love and respect. Together, we must seek the mind of Christ.

As American Baptists we oppose abortion,

- as a means of avoiding responsibility for conception,

- as a primary means of birth control,

- without regard for the far-reaching consequences of the act.

We denounce irresponsible sexual behavior and acts of violence that contribute to the large number of abortions each year.

We grieve with all who struggle with the difficult circumstances that lead them to consider abortion. Recognizing that each person is ultimately responsi-

---

1. Gloria Elaine White-Hammond, MD, and Ray Hammond, MD. "Consideration of the Abortion Issue," in *AME Working Papers*. (Nashville, TN: African Methodist Episcopal Church, 1977), III-18–III-19.

ble to God, we encourage men and women in these circumstances to seek spiritual counsel as they prayerfully and conscientiously consider their decision.

We condemn violence and harassment directed against abortion clinics, their staff and clients, as well as sanctions and discrimination against medical professionals whose consciences prevent them from being involved in abortions.

We acknowledge the diversity of deeply held convictions within our fellowship even as we seek to interpret the Scriptures under the guidance of the Holy Spirit. Many American Baptists believe that, biblically, human life begins at conception, that abortion is immoral and a destruction of a human being created in God's image (Job 31:15; Psalm 139:13–16; Jeremiah 1:5; Luke 1:44; Proverbs 31:8–9; Galatians 1:15). Many others believe that while abortion is a regrettable reality, it can be a morally acceptable action and they choose to act on the biblical principles of compassion and justice (John 8:1–11; Exodus 21:22–25; Matthew 7:1–5; James 2:2–13) and freedom of will (John 16:13; Romans 14:4–5, 10–13). Many gradations of opinion between these basic positions have been expressed within our fellowship.

We also recognize that we are divided as to the proper witness of the church to the state regarding abortion. Many of our membership seek legal safeguards to protect unborn life. Many others advocate for and support family planning legislation, including legalized abortion as in the best interest of women in particular and society in general. Again, we have many points of view between these two positions. Consequently, we acknowledge the freedom of each individual to advocate for a public policy on abortion that reflects his or her beliefs.

Respecting our varied perspectives, let us affirm our unity in the ministry of Christ (Colossians 3:12–17):

- Praying for openness and sensitivity to the leading of the Holy Spirit within our family,

- Covenanting to address both the causes and effects of abortion at the personal and social levels.

We call upon:

American Baptist Congregations

- To challenge members to live in a way that models responsible sexuality in accordance with biblical teaching,

- To expend efforts and funds for teaching responsible sexuality,

- To provide opportunities for intergenerational dialogue on responsible sexuality and Christian life,

- To provide relevant ministries to adolescents and parents of adolescents in and outside the church.

Pastors and Leaders

- To prepare themselves to minister compassionately and skillfully to women and men facing problem pregnancies, whatever their final decisions.

American Baptist Regions

- To provide leadership and support for appropriate programs and ministries to aid the local churches in these tasks.

Seminaries and Institutions of Higher Education

- To provide counsel that will enrich the theological understanding and counseling skills of American Baptist leaders so that they will be able to assist persons facing decisions regarding responsible sexuality and abortion.

National Program Boards

- To assist churches by maintaining a current study packet on abortion which could be helpful to any church's ministry regardless of its position on this subject.

- To prepare, identify and make available other appropriate materials relating to responsible sexuality at all age levels.

We encourage congregations and individual members

- To engage in meaningful dialogue on abortion with openness and Christian compassion,

- To initiate and/or become involved in creative community ministries in their communities that provide alternatives to abortion for women with problem pregnancies and for their loved ones,

- To provide appropriate financial and emotional support for those women who carry their pregnancies to term and further to maintain contact and provide loving community for them after birth,

- To acknowledge that men are equally responsible for the creation of problem pregnancies and to help them to recognize their responsibility for the social, medical, moral and financial consequences of their behavior,

- To minister with love and spiritual counsel to those who choose to terminate their pregnancies,

- To be actively involved in caring for children who are potentially available for adoption, including those with special needs, and to assist agencies in order to facilitate placement for them, and

- To participate in organizations addressing abortion issues in ways that are consistent with their beliefs, and witness to the reconciling love of God.

Beyond our household of faith we call upon:

- Government, industries and foundations to support the research and development of safe, reliable, affordable and culturally appropriate methods of contraception for both men and women worldwide.

- Our governmental institutions to continue to pursue the goals of economic justice, social equality and political empowerment without which the painful human dilemmas now being faced will continue without relief. We are concerned that many women receiving abortions are themselves adolescents who are often economically disadvantaged.

- Public media (television, cinema, audio and print) to stop the depiction of sex outside of marriage as normal and desirable, the portrayal of women, men and children as sex objects and the elevation of sex as the source of all happiness. We particularly oppose print and cinematic pornography.

- We acknowledge that we often lack compassion, insight and the necessary commitment needed to serve our Christian community and the wider society adequately. We affirm our commitment to continue to counsel and uphold one another, to maintain fellowship with those whose opinions differ from ours and to extend the compassion of Christ to all.

- Adopted by the General Board of the American Baptist Churches —June 1988[2]

---

2. Maureen Muldoon, ed. "American Baptist Church Resolution Concerning Abortion and Ministry in the Local Church," in *The Abortion Debate in the United States and Canada: A Source Book.* (New York: Garland Publishing Inc., 1991), 69–74.

ASSEMBLIES OF GOD

Abortion

This document reflects commonly held beliefs based on scripture which have been endorsed by the church's Commission on Doctrinal Purity and the Executive Presbytery.

Why does the Assemblies of God oppose abortion?

The Assemblies of God is unashamedly pro-life. Even though a United States Supreme Court decision legalized abortion in 1973, abortion is still immoral and sinful. This stand is founded on the biblical truth that all human life is created in the image of God (Genesis 1:27). From that truth issues the long-standing Christian view that aborting the life of a developing child is evil.

Those who defend abortion claim that an unborn child in the early stages of development is merely fetal tissue, not a person. But neither science nor medicine can declare an arbitrary time during pregnancy when human life begins. The Bible indicates that human life begins at conception (Job 31:15, Psalm 139:13–16). Because of the sacredness of human life, the matter is settled by theological statement of Scripture, not by a medical determination of viability outside the mother's womb.

There is a Christian alternative to abortion. Instead of terminating the life of the unborn child, the newborn can be placed for adoption by loving Christians. Adoption is a concept authored by God, for all Christian believers have been adopted into the family of God. By choosing to give birth to her baby rather than having an abortion, the birth mother spares the life of a child created in the image of God.

Concerns

Some professing Christians use unchristian methods to oppose abortion. But we must never forget the priority God places on His spiritual and material creation. The soul and where it will spend eternity is of primary importance. Believers must recognize God also loves those who are proabortion, so we must show compassion also. Yet, at the same time, we must try to halt the horrendous murder of innocents in our country.

Just stopping abortions is not enough. The church must show compassion and support toward those who carry their child to birth but do not have the needed resources or an awareness of adoption options.

Because of the advances in medical science, very few mothers today die in pregnancy or childbirth. Yet in some infrequent cases saving the life of the child or of the mother may mean the death of the other. If after prayer for God's intervention, the problem is not resolved, consultation with attending pro-life physicians will be helpful in arriving at the proper conclusion.

The above statement is based upon our common understanding of scriptural teaching. The official delineation of this position is found in the Assemblies of God position paper, "A Biblical Perspective on Abortion," 1985.

All Scripture quotations are from the New International Version (NIV) unless otherwise specified.[3]

CATHOLIC CHURCH

2270 Human life must be respected and protected absolutely from the moment of conception.

> From the first moment of his existence, a human being must be recognized as having the rights of a person—among which is the inviolable right of every innocent being to life.[71]

> Before I formed you in the womb I knew you, and before you were born I consecrated you.[72]

> My frame was not hidden from you, when I was being made in secret, intricately wrought in the depths of the earth.[73]

2271 Since the first century the Church has affirmed the moral evil of every procured abortion. This teaching has not changed and remains unchangeable. Direct abortion, that is to say, abortion willed either as an end or a means, is gravely contrary to the moral law:

> You shall not kill the embryo by abortion and shall not cause the newborn to perish.[74]

> God, the Lord of life, has entrusted to men the noble mission of safeguarding life, and men must carry it out in a manner worthy of themselves. Life must be protected with the utmost care from the moment of conception: abortion and infanticide are abominable crimes.[75]

2272 Formal cooperation in an abortion constitutes a grave offense.

The Church attaches the canonical penalty of excommunication to this crime against human life.

> "A person who procures a completed abortion incurs excommunication latae sententiae," [76] "by the very commission of the offense," [77] and subject to the conditions provided by Canon Law.[78]

3. "Beliefs: Abortion," from the Assemblies of God website. (Springfield, MO, 1985 [cited 3 July 2007]); available from http://ag.org/top/Beliefs/contempissues_01_abortion .cfm; INTERNET.

The Church does not thereby intend to restrict the scope of mercy. Rather, she makes clear the gravity of the crime committed, the irreparable harm done to the innocent who is put to death, as well as to the parents and the whole of society.

2273 The inalienable right to life of every innocent human individual is a constitutive element of a civil society and its legislation:

> "The inalienable rights of the person must be recognized and respected by civil society and the political authority. These human rights depend neither on single individuals nor on parents; nor do they represent a concession made by society and the state; they belong to human nature and are inherent in the person by virtue of the creative act from which the person took his origin. Among such fundamental rights one should mention in this regard every human being's right to life and physical integrity from the moment of conception until death."[79]

> "The moment a positive law deprives a category of human beings of the protection which civil legislation ought to accord them, the state is denying the equality of all before the law. When the state does not place its power at the service of the rights of each citizen, and in particular of the more vulnerable, the very foundations of a state based on law are undermined . . . As a consequence of the respect and protection which must be ensured for the unborn child from the moment of conception, the law must provide appropriate penal sanctions for every deliberate violation of the child's rights."[80]

2274 Since it must be treated from conception as a person, the embryo must be defended in its integrity, cared for, and healed, as far as possible, like any other human being.

Prenatal diagnosis is morally licit, "if it respects the life and integrity of the embryo and the human fetus and is directed toward its safe guarding or healing as an individual . . .

It is gravely opposed to the moral law when this is done with the thought of possibly inducing an abortion, depending upon the results: a diagnosis must not be the equivalent of a death sentence."[81]

2275 "One must hold as licit procedures carried out on the human embryo which respect the life and integrity of the embryo and do not involve disproportionate risks for it, but are directed toward its healing the improvement of its condition of health, or its individual survival."[82]

> "It is immoral to produce human embryos intended for exploitation as disposable biological material."[83] "Certain attempts to influence

chromosomic or genetic inheritance are not therapeutic but are aimed at producing human beings selected according to sex or other predetermined qualities. Such manipulations are contrary to the personal dignity of the human being and his integrity and identity"[84] which are unique and unrepeatable.

71 Cf. CDF, Donum vitae I, 1.

72 Jer 1:5; cf. Job 10:8–12; Ps 22:10–11.

73 Ps 139:15.

74 Didache 2,2: SCh 248, 148; cf. Ep. Barnabae 19,5: PG 2, 777; AD Diognetum 5, 6: PG2, 1173; Tertullian, Apol. 9: PL 1, 319–320.

75 GS 51 par. 3.

76 CIC, can. 1398.

77 CIC, can. 1314.

78 Cf. CIC, cann. 1323–1324.

79 CDF, Donum vitae III.

80 CDF, Donum vitae III.

81 CDF, Donum vitae I, 2.

82 CDF, Donum vitae I, 3.

83 CDF, Donum vitae I, 5.[4]

CHRISTIAN CHURCH—DISCIPLES OF CHRIST

General Assembly Resolutions NO. 0725
(SENSE-OF-THE-ASSEMBLY)
Proactive Prevention: Seeking Common Ground on the Issue of Abortion

WHEREAS, debates over abortion often reflect the division of North American society and of the contemporary church; and

WHEREAS, such debates often fail to address the root causes of abortion; and

WHEREAS, experience shows that it is possible to reduce the number of abortions, while still affirming a woman's privilege to responsibly exercise her inherent freedom of conscience, through programs that provide better health care and community support for women during pregnancy; and

WHEREAS, proactive prevention seeks to find common ground on the issue of abortion by focusing on the prevention of unwanted pregnancies and by supporting pregnant women rather than focusing on the divisive and polarizing debates between pro-choice and pro-life advocates; 1 and

WHEREAS, Christians are called to seek reconciliation within the church whenever possible in order that the church might model reconciliation to the wider society (2 Corinthians 5: 18–19); and

4. *Catechism of the Catholic Church*, 547–49.

WHEREAS, the Christian Church (Disciples of Christ) is particularly called in our Mission Imperative statement "to engage in ministries of reconciliation, compassion, unity and justice" 2 (Ephesians 4:1–3); and

WHEREAS, debates are often marked by caricature and, thus, fail to acknowledge that all Christians affirm the sanctity of life and the dignity of women;

THEREFORE, BE IT RESOLVED that the General Assembly of the Christian Church (Disciples of Christ) meeting in Ft. Worth, Texas, July 21–25, 2007, encourage all manifestations of the church to participate in proactive prevention by:

1. Repenting of the sin of vilifying one another based on our opinions on divisive topics such as abortion or of using such opinions as tests of Christian fellowship or faith.3 (Ephesians 4:31–32)

2. Engaging in age appropriate health and sexuality education paired with Christian spirituality for adults and youth.4

3. Facilitating education for men as to their responsibilities in sexual relationships to ensure the safety and dignity of women and children.

4. Supporting shelters for women and children in crisis pregnancy situations.5

5. Supporting women who have had abortions, or who face difficult decisions regarding pregnancy, by providing our churches as sanctuaries offering healing pastoral and congregational care through compassionate listening and the embodiment of God's gracious presence. (Psalm 46 and 116)

6. Advocating for pregnancy counseling and adequate healthcare for women and families.

7. Advocating for and/or creating affordable daycare facilities in underserved neighborhoods, college campuses and other areas where children and families, have the greatest need.

8. Being an available resource for others by embodying and offering "proactive prevention" as an alternative perspective and model of mission regarding abortion.

9. Witnessing from our doorsteps "to the ends of the earth," to the power of God's reconciling and renewing Spirit in the midst of divisive and polarizing issues confronting God's world. (Acts 1:8).

NOTES:

1. We list General Assembly Resolution No. 7332 as our precedent. Approved October 1973, NO. 7322 resolved the following:

"THEREFORE, BE IT RESOLVED that the General Assembly of the Christian Church (Disciples of Christ) meeting at Cincinnati, Ohio, October 26–31, 1973, strongly encourages individual congregations to give disciplined study to the matter of abortion, calling upon ethical resources of all God's people, contemporary and historical, and upon those disciplines which bear upon it, such as medicine, psychology, and laws.

BE IT FURTHER RESOLVED that persons who must decide whether or not to undergo an abortion shall have the informed supportive resources of the Christian community to help them make responsible choices, and that congregations and individuals give continued full support to each person who must make such a decision, knowing that whether or not an abortion is decided the person will need the supportive assurance of God's grace and love which meaningfully can come with the Christian community."

General Assembly Resolution No. 24, approved August 1975, resolved the following:

"THEREFORE, BE IT RESOLVED, that the General Assembly of the Christian Church (Disciples of Christ) meeting at San Antonio, Texas, August 15–20, 1975.

• Affirm the principle of individual liberty, freedom of individual conscience, and sacredness of life for all persons.

• Respect differences in religious beliefs concerning abortion and oppose, in accord with the principle of religious liberty, any attempt to legislate a specific religious opinion or belief concerning abortion upon all Americans,

• Provide through ministry of the local congregation, pastoral concern, and nurture of persons faced with the responsibility and trauma surrounding undesired pregnancy."

2. Mission Imperative of the Christian Church (Disciples of Christ) adopted July 2000.

3. In the "Declaration and Address" of the "Christian Association of Washington" of 1809, Thomas Campbell expresses the following: "Moreover, being well aware, as from sad experience, of the heinous nature and pernicious tendency of religious controversy among Christians; tired and sick of the bitter jarrings and janglings of a party spirit, we would desire to be at rest; and were it possible, we would also desire to adopt and recommend such measures as would give rest to our brethren [sisters and brothers] throughout all the churches; as would restore unity, peace, and purity to the whole Church of God."

4. "Our Whole Lives" and "Sexuality and Our Faith" are two interrelated curriculum prepared in part by our ecumenical partner the UCC to address this need. Training for the curriculum is required. Information about this program can be found on the United Church of Christ website at http://www.ucc.org/justice/owl/ or by calling 216-736-3718.

5. For more information about the NBA's Olive Branch call (314) 381-3100. A wish list of items which congregations can supply to Olive Branch can be found on the NBA website at http://www.nbacares.org/.

SCRIPTURAL REFERENCES: (New Revised Standard Version) Matthew 12:25— "Every kingdom divided against itself is laid waste, and no city or house divided against itself will stand"

2 Corinthians 5:18–19—"All this is from God, who reconciled us to himself through Christ, and has given us the ministry of reconciliation; that is, in Christ God was reconciling the world to himself."

Ephesians 4:1–3—"I . . . beg you to lead a life worthy of the calling to which you have been called, with all humility and gentleness, with patience, bearing with one another in love, making every effort to maintain the unity of the Spirit in the bond of peace."

Ephesians 4:31–32—"Put away from you all bitterness and wrath and anger and wrangling and slander, together with all malice, and be kind to one another, tenderhearted, forgiving one another, as God in Christ has forgiven you."

Luke 4:18—"the Spirit of the Lord is upon me, because he has anointed me to bring good news to the poor . . ."

Psalm 46—"God is our refuge and strength, a very present help in trouble . . .ff."

Psalm 116—"I love the Lord because he has heard my voice and my supplications . . .ff."

Acts 1:8—"But you will receive power when the Holy Spirit has come upon you; and you will be my witnesses to the ends of the earth"

Compton Heights Christian Church, St. Louis, MO

The General Board recommends that the General Assembly ADOPT Business Item No. 0725. (Debate time 12 minutes).[5]

CHURCH OF THE NAZARENE

C. Sanctity of Human Life

36. The Church of the Nazarene believes in the sanctity of human life and strives to protect against abortion, embryonic stem cell research, euthanasia, and the withholding of reasonable medical care to handicapped or elderly.

Induced Abortion. The Church of the Nazarene affirms the sanctity of human life as established by God the Creator and believes that such sanctity extends to the child not yet born. Life is a gift from God. All human life, including life developing in the womb, is created by God in His image and is, therefore, to be nurtured, supported, and protected. From the moment of conception, a child is a human being with all of the developing characteristics of human life, and this life is dependent on the mother for its continued development. Therefore, we believe that human life must be respected and protected from the moment of conception. We oppose induced abortion by any means, when used for either personal convenience or population control. We oppose laws that allow abortion. Realizing that there are rare, but real medical conditions wherein the mother or the unborn child, or both, could not survive the pregnancy, termination of the pregnancy should only be made after sound medical and Christian counseling. Responsible opposition to abortion requires our commitment to the initiation and support of programs designed to provide care for mothers and children. The crisis of an unwanted pregnancy calls for the community of believers (represented only by those for whom knowledge of the crisis is ap-

5. "General Assembly Resolution NO. 0725 (Sense-of-the-Assembly) Proactive Prevention: Seeking Common Ground on the Issue of Abortion," from the Christian Church—Disciples of Christ website. (Indianapolis, IN, 2007 [cited 15 Aug. 2007]); available from http://www.disciples.org/ga/resolutions/0725/; INTERNET.

propriate) to provide a context of love, prayer, and counsel. In such instances, support can take the form of counseling centers, homes for expectant mothers, and the creation or utilization of Christian adoption services.

The Church of the Nazarene recognizes that consideration of abortion as a means of ending an unwanted pregnancy often occurs because Christian standards of sexual responsibility have been ignored. Therefore the church calls for persons to practice the ethic of the New Testament as it bears upon human sexuality and to deal with the issue of abortion by placing it within the larger framework of biblical principles that provide guidance for moral decision making. (Genesis 2:7, 9:6; Exodus 20:13; 21:12–16, 22–25; Leviticus 18:21; Job 31:15; Psalms 22:9; 139:3–16; Isaiah 44:2, 24; 49:5; Jeremiah 1:5; Luke 1:15, 23–25, 36–45; Acts 17:25; Romans 12:1–2; 1 Corinthians 6:16; 7:1ff.; 1 Thessalonians 4:3–6)

The Church of the Nazarene also recognizes that many have been affected by the tragedy of abortion. Each local congregation and individual believer is urged to offer the message of forgiveness by God for each person who has experienced abortion. Our local congregations are to be communities of redemption and hope to all who suffer physical, emotional, and spiritual pain as a result of the willful termination of a pregnancy. (Romans 3:22–24; Galatians 6:1)[6]

CONSERVATIVE CONGREGATIONAL CHRISTIAN CONFERENCE

Statement On Abortion

Christians affirm that human yearning for reality and meaning can be satisfied only by the knowledge of and a relationship with a personal God who alone can change human nature and liberate from the bondage of self-indulgence. (1) Human worth is a consequence of being made by and in the image of a personal God (2) who is sovereign over history and places us within the framework of God's continual acts in history. (3) The dominant philosophy of this age opposes this world and life view and asserts the dignity and worth of people and their capacity for self-realization through reason apart from the supernatural and sovereign involvement of a personal God. (4) Clear lines of confrontation between these two opposing faiths are not always easily discerned by the Christian community, both individually and corporately. Cultural conditioning, ignorance of God's revealed will and sin all mitigate against a clear perception of many ethical and moral issues. Nevertheless, we affirm the authority and witness of God's revelation in Scripture and the heritage of Church history regarding the dignity and sanctity of all human life and oppose anything that

6. *Manual of the Church of the Nazarene 2005–2009*, 53–54.

would blur or lessen its value. (5) We humbly recognize the complex presuppositions, realities and implications of ethical/moral decision-making and confess our own sinful silence in failing to act where the lines of conflict are obvious. (6) We accept the challenge to confront the pragmatism of this age and seek to move away from past indifferences and the subtle seductive power of this age. (7) We, therefore, affirm that abortion on demand for reasons such as personal convenience, social adjustment, economic advantage, genetic defect, or physical malformation is morally wrong. (8)

Statement

We believe that all human life is a gift from God and is therefore sacred. (9) The Lord has created all life sacred and cherishes all lives: including all those which have been marked by the effects of the fall of nature, resulting in physical and mental abnormalities. (10) We believe that God has told us, in Scripture, what our attitude should be towards the unborn.(11) Specific blessings have been conferred upon unborn infants, pre-eminently in the incarnation of Jesus Christ.(12) Scripture clearly states that God provided penalties for actions which result in the death of the unborn.(13) The fetus is not a growth or piece of tissue in the mother's body, nor even a potential human being, but a human life who, though not yet mature, is growing into the fullness of the humanity it already possesses.(14) The humanness of the fetus is con-firmed by modern medical science. From the moment of conception a unique genetic code distinct from both parents is established, sex is determined and the only requirements for development into an adult human being are time and nutrition. Thus, we affirm that the moral issue of abortion is more than a question of the freedom of a woman to control the reproductive functions of her body. It is a question of moral responsibility involving at least two human beings at different stages of maturity. Abortion transcends issues of personal, economic and social convenience or compassion. No woman gives birth to herself. She gives birth to a child that is a distinct body and personality from herself. Consequently, even if we agree that every woman has a right to do with her own body as she sees fit, (15) we cannot conclude that she therefore has the right to take the life of her child. However, in the rare situation when the life of the unborn child mortally threatens the equal life of the mother, the mother is not required to sacrifice her life. (16) We believe that the Church is commissioned to declare and demonstrate this high regard for human life, the reality and complexity of the sinful human condition and God's forgiveness through grace and the redemptive work of Jesus Christ. (17) The community of Christian believers furnishes the context out of which this declaration and demonstration grow. (18) It is the responsibility of the Church to insist that society not adopt a policy that would deny the sanctity of human life and lead people to take life lightly. The Church must advocate the protection of the freedom of those who cannot protect themselves. The Church must therefore seek to protect the un-born child's freedom to live. (19) In addition, Christians must reach out to those who are confronted with the crisis for which abortion seems a solution with the offer of a Biblical alternative, providing the practical care and compassion needed. (20)

Conclusion

The Gospel of Jesus Christ is the only adequate answer to the terrible spiritual, moral and social dilemma confronting the society that legalizes abortion and the parents contemplating abortion. Christians are called to live in active tension with culture, neither becoming complacent toward evil nor proponents of it but promoting the truth of God's revelation. (21) The current state of affairs in our society compels Christians to share in the responsibility for the tragedy upon us, to promote justice and propagate the promises of grace. (22) Christians have a responsibility to be involved in the legislative process of our democratic society for the purpose of guarding the freedom of the unborn. The Church also has the obligation to educate its own constitutents and society itself concerning the complex issues surrounding abortion and equip people with a Biblical alternative. (24) God has commissioned the Church to experience and express the redemption that is available in Christ Jesus. Therefore, it is precisely to those who are in trouble and despair that the Church has to present the message of forgiveness and redemption. Even those who have sinned must be sheltered by Christian love and assured that no one is beyond the scope of God's forgiveness. (25) The Church must also create alternatives and share the burden of caring for the lives of those brought into the world under difficult circumstances. (26) May God's grace and wisdom prevail as we seek to work for an end to abortion.

INDEX OF SCRIPTURE REFERENCES

(1.) Phil. 3:8–11; I Cor. 6:9–11 (2.) Ps. 139:14; Gen. 1:26,27 (3.) Job 38:4; Is.9:6,7; 11:1–9; 46:9,10; (4.) Gen. 4:11,12; Rom. 1:18–32; Ps. 72:1–11; 2 Pet. 3:11–14 I Cor. 1:18–20; 2:14 (5. Prov. 14:34; 29:18; Mt. 28:18,20 (6.) Prov. 24:11,12 (7.) Eph. 2:2; 2 Cor. 4:3,4 (8.) Ex. 20:13 (9.) Ps. 127:3; 139:13–16 (10.) Ex. 4:11; Jn 9:1–3 (11.) Ex. 21:22,23 (NIV) (12.) Jer. 1:5; Lk. 1:15; Gal. 1:15; Mt. 1:20 (13.) Ex. 21:22–25 (14.) Job 10:8a,10–12 (15.) 1 Cor. 6:13b,l9,20 (16.) Ex. 22:2,3; Jn. 15:12,13 (17.) Ps. 32:1,2; Rom. 5:1,6–11 (18.) I Jn. 3:11–22 (19.) Mt. 25:40,45; 28:18–20; (20.) Jas.1:27; 2:14–17; Ps. 106:3 Prov. 24:11,12; Amos 5:15,24 (21.) Mt. 5:10–16; Heb. 11:36–38 (22.) Gen. 1:28a; Mt. 28:18–20; Mk. 16:15 (23.) 1 Tim. 1:8–11 (24.) Hos. 4:1–6 (25.) 1 Jn. 1:9; Mk. 3:28 (26.) Jas. 1:27; 2:14–17; I Jn. 3:17[7]

7. "CCCC Position Papers: Statement On Abortion," from the Conservative Congregational Christian Conference website. (Lake Elmo, MN [cited 27 June 2007]);

EPISCOPAL CHURCH USA

Resolution Number 1994-A054
Title: Reaffirm Gerbneral Convention Statement on Childbrith and Abortion
Legislative Action Taken: Concurred as Substituted and Amended

Resolved, the House of Bishops concurring, That this 71st General Convention of the Episcopal Church reaffirms resolution C047 from the 69th General Convention, which states:

All human life is sacred from its inception until death. The Church takes seriously its obligation to help form the consciences of its members concerning this sacredness. Human life, therefore, should be initiated only advisedly and in full accord with this understanding of the power to conceive and give birth which is bestowed by God. It is the responsibility of our congregations to assist their members in becoming informed concerning the spiritual and physiological aspects of sex and sexuality.

The Book of Common Prayer affirms that "the birth of a child is a joyous and solemn occasion in the life of a family. It is also an occasion for rejoicing in the Christian community" (p. 440). As Christians we also affirm responsible family planning.

We regard all abortion as having a tragic dimension, calling for the concern and compassion of all the Christian community.

While we acknowledge that in this country it is the legal right of every woman to have a medically safe abortion, as Christians we believe strongly that if this right is exercised, it should be used only in extreme situations. We emphatically oppose abortion as a means of birth control, family planning, sex selection, or any reason of mere convenience.

In those cases where an abortion is being considered, members of this Church are urged to seek the dictates of their conscience in prayer, to seek the advice and counsel of members of the Christian community and where appropriate, the sacramental life of this Church.

Whenever members of this Church are consulted with regard to a problem pregnancy, they are to explore, with grave seriousness, with the person or persons seeking advice and counsel, as alternatives to abortion, other positive courses of action, including, but not limited to, the following possibilities: the parents raising the child; another family member raising the child; making the child available for adoption.

It is the responsibility of members of this Church, especially the clergy, to become aware of local agencies and resources which will assist those faced with problem pregnancies.

available from http://www.ccccusa.com/files/CCCCPositionPapers.pdf; INTERNET.

We believe that legislation concerning abortions will not address the root of the problem. We therefore express our deep conviction that any proposed legislation on the part of national or state governments regarding abortions must take special care to see that the individual conscience is respected, and that the responsibility of individuals to reach informed decisions in this matter is acknowledged and honored as the position of this Church; and be it further

Resolved, That this 71st General Convention of the Episcopal Church express its unequivocal opposition to any legislative, executive or judicial action on the part of local, state or national governments that abridges the right of a woman to reach an informed decision about the termination of pregnancy or that would limit the access of a woman to safe means of acting on her decision.[8]

EVANGELICAL CONGREGATIONAL CHURCH

143.1.2.5 Abortion

The moral issue of abortion is more than a question of the freedom of a woman to control the reproductive functions of her own body. It is a question of those circumstances under which a human being may be permitted to take the life of another.

Since life is a gift of God, neither the life of an unborn child nor the life of the mother may be lightly taken.

The value of life prior to birth is seen throughout the Scriptures (Psalms 139:13–16; 51:5; Jeremiah 1:5; Luke 1:41–44). Divine blessing is conferred upon an unborn infant (Luke 1:42, "Blessed is the child you will bear!"). The strife-filled lives of Jacob and Esau are shown already in process prior to birth (Genesis 25:22–23).

It is neither right nor proper to terminate a pregnancy solely on the basis of personal convenience or sociological considerations. Abortion on demand for social adjustment or to solve economic problems is morally wrong. On those rare occasions when abortion may seem morally justified, the decision should be made only after there has been thorough and sensitive religious, medical, and psychological consultation and counseling.[9]

---

8. "Resolution Number 1994-A054," General Convention, *Journal of the General Convention of . . . The Episcopal Church*, Indianapolis, 1994 (New York: General Convention, 1995), 323–25.

9. "Moral Standards: Abortion," from the Evangelical Congregational Church website. (Myerstown, PA [cited 27 June 2007]); available from http://www.eccenter.com/files/ecc/publications/discipline/moral_standards.pdf; INTERNET.

EVANGELICAL LUTHERAN CHURCH OF AMERICA

From "Abortion"

IV. A. Continuing the Pregnancy

Because of the Christian presumption to preserve and protect life, this church, in most circumstances, encourages women with unintended pregnancies to continue the pregnancy. Faith and trust in God's promises has the power to sustain people in the face of seemingly insurmountable obstacles. In each set of circumstances, there must also be a realistic assessment of what will be necessary to bear, nurture, and provide for children over the long-term, and what resources are available or need to be provided for this purpose. The needs of children are a constant. The parenting arrangements through which these needs are met may vary. If it is not possible for both parents to raise the child, this might be done by one parent, by the extended family, or by foster or adoptive parents.

This church encourages and seeks to support adoption as a positive option to abortion. Because adoption is an increasingly more open process today, it generally is easier for birth parents to have a role in selecting the adoptive parents and in maintaining some contact with the child. These possibilities can be helpful in the grieving process that is likely to occur when birth parent(s) choose to place the child for adoption after having bonded with the child during pregnancy. Care needs to be taken in selecting adoption processes that do not exploit but safeguard the welfare of all parties involved. At the same time, we recognize that there are unintended pregnancies for which adoption is not an acceptable option.

We encourage and seek to make it possible for people of diverse cultural and racial backgrounds and with limited financial means to adopt children. We encourage those who contemplate adopting to consider adopting children with special needs. Mothers and fathers choosing to place their children for adoption should be affirmed and supported in view of society's prejudices against such decisions.

B. Ending a Pregnancy

This church recognizes that there can be sound reasons for ending a pregnancy through induced abortion. The following provides guidance for those considering such a decision. We recognize that conscientious decisions need to be made in relation to difficult circumstances that vary greatly. What is determined to be a morally responsible decision in one situation may not be in another.

In reflecting ethically on what should be done in the case of an unintended pregnancy, consideration should be given to the status and condition of the life in the womb. We also need to consider the conditions under which the pregnancy occurred and the implications of the pregnancy for the woman's life.

An abortion is morally responsible in those cases in which continuation of a pregnancy presents a clear threat to the physical life of the woman.

A woman should not be morally obligated to carry the resulting pregnancy to term if the pregnancy occurs when both parties do not participate willingly in sexual intercourse.[E] This is especially true in cases of rape and incest. This can also be the case in some situations in which women are so dominated and oppressed that they have no choice regarding sexual intercourse and little access to contraceptives. Some conceptions occur under dehumanizing conditions that are contrary to God's purposes.

There are circumstances of extreme fetal abnormality, which will result in severe suffering and very early death of an infant. In such cases, after competent medical consultations, the parent(s) may responsibly choose to terminate the pregnancy. Whether they choose to continue or to end such pregnancies, this church supports the parent(s) with compassion, recognizing the struggle involved in the decision.

Although abortion raises significant moral issues at any stage of fetal development, the closer the life in the womb comes to full term the more serious such issues become.[F] When a child can survive outside a womb, it becomes possible for other people, and not only the mother, to nourish and care for the child. This church opposes ending intrauterine life when a fetus is developed enough to live outside a uterus with the aid of reasonable and necessary technology. If a pregnancy needs to be interrupted after this point, every reasonable and necessary effort should be made to support this life, unless there are lethal fetal abnormalities indicating that the prospective newborn will die very soon.

Our biblical and confessional commitments provide the basis for us to continue deliberating together on the moral issues related to these decisions. We have the responsibility to make the best possible decisions in light of the information available to us and our sense of accountability to God, neighbor, and self. In these decisions, we must ultimately rely on the grace of God.

Addendum

The following amendments (at the points indicated in the text) received significant support at the Churchwide Assembly but they did not receive the vote needed for approval:

[D] to insert a new paragraph at this point: "The support given by members of this church will seek to witness to the scriptural norm that God is the creator and preserver of life. This church, and especially the pastors, will carry out its ministry with both God's Law and God's Gospel, and proclaim forgiveness and new life to all who are troubled and penitent."

[E] "A woman should not be morally obligated to carry the resulting pregnancy to term if the pregnancy occurs in cases of rape and incest."

[F] "Abortion is not acceptable later than the first trimester."

[G] "The Church must work vigorously to support state and national legislation to provide free prenatal and maternity care to women whose medical needs are not adequately met through medical insurance."[10]

EVANGELICAL PRESBYTERIAN CHURCH

On Abortion

The Evangelical Presbyterian Church is convinced that the Bible strongly affirms the dignity and value of every human life.

> *"Before I formed you in the womb I knew you, and before you were born I consecrated you; I appointed you a prophet to the nations."* (**Jeremiah** 1:5)

> *"My frame was hidden from Thee when I was being made in secret, intricately wrought in the depths of the earth."* (**Psalm** 139:15)

> *"Listen to me, O coastlands, and hearken, you peoples from afar. The Lord called me from the womb, from the body of my mother He named me."* (**Isaiah** 49:1)

> *"For he will be great in the sight of the Lord, and he will drink no wine or liquor; and he will be filled with the Holy Spirit while yet in his mother's womb."* (**Luke** 1:15)

> *"And when Elizabeth heard the greeting of Mary, the babe leaped in her womb; and Elizabeth was filled with the Holy Spirit."* (**Luke** 1:41)

The Westminster Shorter Catechism, a confessional statement shared by most Reformed churches, forbids the taking of life while demanding the preservation of life:

> *"The Sixth Commandment requireth all lawful endeavors to preserve our own life, and the life of others."* (**Question** 68)

> *"The Sixth Commandment forbiddeth the taking away of our own life, or the life of our neighbor unjustly, or whatsoever tendeth thereunto."* (**Question** 69)

---

10. "Abortion," by the Department for Studies, Division for Church in Society from the Evangelical Lutheran Church of America website. (Chicago, IL, Sept. 1991 [cited 27 June 2007]); available from http://www.elca.org/SocialStatements/abortion/; INTERNET.

Scripture teaches that we are not merely to avoid involvement in injustice. God's people are called upon to speak for the oppressed and defenseless. The Scripture passages cited above are evidence that God accords human value and dignity to the unborn child.

The 6th General Assembly of the Evangelical Presbyterian Church affirms that the Bible does not distinguish between prenatal and postnatal life. It attributes human personhood to the unborn child.

Because we hold these convictions concerning unborn children, we urge the promotion of legislation that brings our judicial and legal systems into line with the scriptural view on protecting the poor and weak.

Christians are called to be good citizens by impacting the state in positive ways. All citizens, Christians and non-Christians alike, must have freedom of conscience on all private moral and ethical issues, since God alone is Lord of the conscience. But the issue of equal protection of life under the laws of the state is not a private but a public matter.

The Bible teaches that all persons and nations are responsible before God for their ethical decisions, including those which relate to the preservation of human life.

In addition to prayers and general assistance, that the General Assembly urges that the following steps be implemented by individuals, congregations, and judicatories in an effort to provide substantial support for those impacted by problem pregnancies:

1. Women facing problem or unwanted pregnancies should receive support, love, acceptance and counsel from pastors, counselors, physicians and Christian friends both during and after the decisions they face. The Church must provide compassionate biblical and spiritual guidance to these persons.

2. The men involved who respond with indifference must be confronted with their responsibilities and role in such crises.

3. The Church must support and nurture women who decide to carry an unwanted pregnancy to full term.

4. The Church must seek ways to support and care for all children who result from unwanted pregnancies.

5. The Church must serve as a therapeutic community to those who have experienced physical, emotional, or spiritual wounds from abortion or giving up a child for adoption.

6. Both individual Christians and the Church should oppose abortion and do everything in their power to provide supportive communities and alternatives to abortion.

7. The Church should declare to the world and teach its members that abortion must never be used as a convenience or a means of birth control.

The purpose of this statement is pastoral. It is best proclaimed by those who are profoundly aware of their continuous need for the mercy and forgiveness of God. The Church must always follow the compassionate example of Christ who said, "Neither do I condemn you. Go and sin no more."

Adopted by the 6th General Assembly, June 1986[11]

GREEK ORTHODOX ARCHDIOCESE
OF NORTH AND SOUTH AMERICA
From "A Statement on Abortion"

It has been the position of the Orthodox Church over the centuries that the taking of unborn life is morally wrong. This is based upon divine law which is the most difficult law for man to comprehend for it transcends the boundaries of human frailty due to its source of divine authority. No law is perfect, and man in his diverse interpretations of the law is continually reminded of his human limitations. Even in such basic law as "Thou Shalt Not Kill": we can take no pride in its exceptions which justify war and self-defense, for they serve only to becloud our unceasing efforts toward shaping man in the image of God. This same principle of exception also extends to the unborn child. When the unborn child places the life of its mother in jeopardy, then and only then can this life be sacrificed for the welfare of its mother. To move beyond this exception would be transgressing man's duty in the protection of human life as understood and interpreted by the Orthodox Church.[12]

---

11. "On Abortion," from Position Papers and Pastoral Letters on the Evangelical Presbyterian Church website. (June 1996 [cited 2 August 2007]); available from http://www.epc.org/about-epc/position-papers/abortion.html; INTERNET.

12. Muldoon, ed. "Greek Orthodox Archdiocese of North and South America: A Statement on Abortion," in *The Abortion Debate in the United States and Canada: A Source Book.* (New York: Garland Publishing Inc., 1991), 86.

THE INTERNATIONAL COMMUNION OF THE CHARISMATIC EPISCOPAL CHURCH

A Declaration on the Sanctity of Human Life, House of Bishops, February 27, 2002

God alone has absolute dominion over human life, and over the process by which it comes into being. The human being is to be respected and treated as a person from the moment of fertilization, that is, the union of an ovum and sperm. The respect and protection of ALL innocent human life is necessary for the establishment and maintenance of a moral civilization.

The Church has the duty and the obligation to proclaim to all the earth the sanctity of human life, the dignity of human life, and respect for human life.

- Human life begins at conception and ends with natural death.

- The deliberate destruction of innocent persons, preborn or born, through all forms of direct abortion, infanticide, euthanasia or any other means is considered to be unethical, immoral, evil and sinful.

Therefore, we affirm that no government has the right to alter the law of God.

- Any legislation by any government that demeans or goes contrary to the law of God concerning the sanctity of life is immoral.

- We affirm the teaching of Holy Scripture and the tradition of the church throughout the centuries that God is the giver of life and thus human life belongs to Him.

We affirm that the destruction of the human embryo, as an end or a means, such as embryonic stem cell research, is unethical, immoral, intrinsically evil, and sinful. The artificial creation of human life through cloning is also unethical, immoral, intrinsically evil, and sinful.

We affirm that this declaration on the sanctity of human life, which is rooted in the teaching of the church and the Holy Scriptures, is not in conflict with good and moral science.[13]

---

13. Charles Jones and Terry Gensemer, "A Declaration on the Sanctity of Human Life," from The International Communion of the Charismatic Episcopal Church website. (San Clemente, CA, February 27, 2002 [cited 27 June 2007]); available from http://www .iccec.org/iccecnews/houseof_bishops/declarations/sanctityhumanlife_feb2002.html; INTERNET.

LUTHERAN CHURCH—MISSOURI SYNOD

The LCMS believes that abortion is contrary to God's Word and "is not a moral option, except as a tragically unavoidable byproduct of medical procedures necessary to prevent the death of another human being, viz., the mother" (1979 Res. 3-02A).[14]

MORAVIAN CHURCH—NORTHERN PROVINCE

From "Abortion"

Whereas, it must be our goal as a denomination to seek deeper spiritual truths concerning social issues and not merely to be aligned with one side on the issue of abortion, and

Whereas, we respect the inevitability of differences of opinion, and respect the personal faith and commitment which underlies the varieties of Christian interpretations, beliefs, and practices, within and beyond the Moravian Church, and

Whereas, the Moravian statement on abortion has been carefully developed over a period of twenty years by Provincial Synods and comprehensively stated by the 1974 Provincial Synod, and

Whereas, abortion continues to be an issue of serious concern for people of faith, for congregations, and for the Northern Province of the Moravian Church, especially in regard to the Northern Province's membership in the Religious Coalition for Abortion Rights, and

Whereas, resolutions from District Synods, both supporting and opposing the Province's membership in RCAR, have been submitted to this Synod, and

Whereas, our unity is rooted in Jesus Christ, not in uniformity of beliefs and practices, therefore be it

RESOLVED: The 1990 Synod of the Moravian Church, Northern Province, reaffirms the 1974 Provincial Synod statement on abortion; and be it further

RESOLVED: The 1990 Synod of the Moravian Church, Northern Province, recommends the use in congregations and for pastoral care the study paper authorized by the Provincial Elders' Conference entitled "Abortion: A Pastoral Perspective;" and be it further

---

14. "Frequently Asked Questions>Moral and Ethical Issues>Life Issues>Abortion," from the Lutheran Church—Missouri Synod website. (St. Louis, MO, 2003–2007 [cited 27 June 2007]); available from http://www.lcms.org/pages/internal.asp?NavID=2120; INTERNET.

RESOLVED: The Moravian Church, Northern Province, shall withdraw its membership from the Religious Coalition for Abortion Rights and direct the Standing Committee on Church and Society to explore membership in RCAR as a committee and, following consultation with the Provincial Elders' Conference, the committee shall determine its relationship with RCAR.

R&E 1990, p. 46, R. 14Ð16

Whereas, "the Moravian Church believes in the sacredness of life and the quality of life. We believe that abortion should not be used as a method of birth control nor as a means of controlling population and that abortion should not be taken lightly or without thorough consideration of alternatives and professional counseling:" (1974 Northern Provincial Synod), and

Whereas, the Moravian Church has had a tradition of leaving decisions regarding moral issues that are not clearly defined in the Bible to individual conscience, and

Whereas, a statement addressing the issue of abortion was made by the 1974 Provincial Synod of the Northern Province of the Moravian Church leaving the decision concerning an unwanted pregnancy to individual conscience, and

Whereas, there is a strong movement in the United States to terminate the freedom to choose abortion, and

Whereas, we respect differences in religious beliefs concerning abortion and oppose, in accord with the principle of religious liberty, any legislation which would stipulate a specific religious opinion or belief concerning abortion upon all Americans (1982 Western District Synod), therefore be it

RESOLVED: that the Moravian Church, Northern Province, affirm its belief in the sacredness of life and the quality of life, its belief that abortion should not be used as a method of birth control nor as a means of controlling population, and its belief that abortion should not be taken lightly or without thorough consideration of alternatives and professional counseling, but that the Moravian Church, Northern Province, join with 30 other religious organizations in the Religious Coalition for Abortion Rights, in order to oppose legislation which would make all abortions illegal.

R&E 1986, pp. 35–36, R. 12

RESOLVED: that this Synod of the Northern Province, respecting the position of our Church regarding abortion as expressed by the 1974 Synod, continue to affirm the sacredness of life and the complex nature of decisions concerning abortion, and as a result record our opposition to a constitutional amendment banning all abortions.

R&E 1982, p. 50, R. 32

Whereas, the Moravian Church believes in the sacredness of life and in the quality of life, and

Whereas, we believe that abortion should not be used as a method of birth control nor a means of controlling population, and

Whereas, Christian faith calls us to affirm the freedom of persons as well as the sanctity of life, therefore be it

RESOLVED: that abortion should be a matter of responsible personal decision, with continuing counseling provided if desired, and be it further

RESOLVED: that alternatives to abortion be given careful consideration in the perspective of possibly bringing mercy to a difficult situation. These alternatives include: (a) adoption, (b) single parenthood, (c) continued pregnancy for a married couple confronted with an unplanned pregnancy, (d) marriage for a single woman, or (e) temporary foster care, and be it further

RESOLVED: that abortion be accepted as an option only where all other possible alternatives will lead to greater destruction of human life and spirit.

Whereas, neither science nor religion has claimed to fully understand the mystery of life or reached a decision as to when the life of an individual begins, and

Whereas, the Bible does not speak directly to the matter of abortion and the Moravian Church has refrained from being dogmatic when a biblical position was not clear, and

Whereas, there are circumstances under which the completion of an unwanted pregnancy may bring physical and/or emotional problems to the child and/or its parent(s), therefore be it

RESOLVED: that members of the Moravian Church view abortion in the perspective of possibly bringing mercy to a difficult situation, and be it further

RESOLVED: that this Synod recommend that any person(s) considering abortion as a possible solution seek qualified medical and spiritual counsel, and be it further

RESOLVED: that the individual(s) who chooses an alternative to abortion be offered adequate counseling during pregnancy and following delivery.

Whereas, it is the mission of the church to minister to persons in need, therefore be it

RESOLVED: that the Moravian Church encourage its members to accept with empathy persons who are dealing with an unwanted pregnancy, and in accord with convictions assist in all possible tangible ways.

R&E 1974, pp. 55–57, R. 9-15

Whereas, recent changes in laws liberalizing abortion make it imperative that the Moravian Church formulate a statement on the issue of abortion; and

Whereas, the Bible does not speak directly to the issues of abortion and neither condemns or condones the act, and since the Moravian Church has maintained a position of refraining from being dogmatic when a Biblical position is not clear; therefore be it

RESOLVED: that this Synod affirm that the decision to interrupt a pregnancy, consistent within the time limit recognized by the medical profession, be the responsibility of the individual(s) involved, based on her interpretation of Christian teaching, and that those who seek such an irreversible alternative do so with considerable thought and adequate medical and spiritual counseling; and

RESOLVED: that abortions should be viewed in the perspective of bringing mercy to a difficult situation where other options may be more destructive; and

Whereas, abortion has been suggested as one means of population control; and

Whereas, this Synod feels that this approach to population control is not in keeping with the above resolutions, therefore be it

RESOLVED: that abortion should not be used as a means of population control.

R&E 1970, pp. 49–50 and ERRATUM, R. 7Ð9

Abbreviations

JNP   Journal of the Provincial Synod (of year indicated)

R&E   Resolutions and Elections of the Provincial Synod of the Northern Province of the Moravian Church (of the year indicated)

R   Resolution number as noted in Journal or Resolutions and Elections[15]

15. "Resolutions/Abortion," from the Moravian Church–Northern Province website. (Bethlehem, PA, 2000 [cited 15 Aug. 2007]); available from http://www.mcnp.org/Documents/Resolutions/Abortion.asp; INTERNET.

ORTHODOX CHURCH IN AMERICA

From the 9th All American Council of the Orthodox Church in America
General Statement

"WHEREAS abortion in all cases has been condemned by the Orthodox
Church in America unequivocally on the basis of Orthodox theology, which
faithfully reflects for today nearly two thousand years of Christian doctrine and
ethical teaching; and . . .

BE IT THEREFORE RESOLVED THAT the 9th American Council of the
Orthodox Church in America strongly reaffirms the Orthodox Church's opposition to abortion in all cases, and that it does so on theological and moral
grounds; commends the efforts of Orthodox bishops, clergy, and laity to bear
witness to the sanctity of life in the public arena, especially noting in this con-
nection the work and witness of Orthodox Christians for Life; and commits the
Orthodox Church in America to continued witness on behalf of the God-given
sanctity of life . . . the Orthodox Church in America recognizes . . . [the] opposition to and condemnation of abortion in all cases, except to save the life of
the mother."[16]

An affirmation from the 10th All American Council of the Orthodox Church
in America to be distributed to Orthodox parishes on Sanctity of Life Sunday,
Jan 18, 1998.

Synodal Affirmation on Abortion

Abortion is an act of murder for which those involved, voluntarily and invol-
untarily, will answer to God.

Those finding themselves confronted with tragic circumstances where
the lives of the mothers and their unborn children are threatened, and where
painful decisions of life and death have to be made—such as those involving
rape, incest and sickness—are to be counseled to take responsible action before
God, Who is both merciful and just, to Whom they will give account for their
actions.

Women and men, including family members and friends of pregnant
women considering abortions, are to be encouraged to resist this evil act, and
be assisted in bearing and raising their children in healthy physical and spiritual conditions.

16. Maureen Muldoon, ed. "9th All American Council of the Orthodox Church in
America, Sept 19–24, 1989, General Statement," in *The Abortion Debate in the United
States and Canada: A Source Book.* (New York: Garland Publishing Inc., 1991), 86.

Women who have had recourse to abortion, men who have fathered aborted children, and others involved in cases of abortion, are to be provided with pastoral care which includes recognition of the gravity of the act and assurance of the mercy of God upon those who repent of their sins.

Orthodox Christians are to contribute to legislative processes according to their knowledge, competence, ability and influence, so that laws may be enacted and enforced which protect and defend the lives of unborn children while being sensitive to the complexities and tragedies of life in contemporary society.[17]

ORTHODOX PRESBYTERIAN CHURCH

Statement on Abortion

Adopted by the thirty-ninth General Assembly of the Orthodox Presbyterian Church (1972)

Believing that unborn children are living creatures in the image of God, given by God as a blessing to their parents, we therefore affirm that voluntary abortion, except possibly to save the physical life of the mother, is in violation of the Sixth Commandment (Exodus 20:13). We state the following reasons:

1. The Bible treats human personhood as beginning at conception (Psalm 139:13–16; 51:5; Jeremiah 1:4,5; Luke 1:14–44; 1:29–38; Exodus 21:22–25).

2. The Bible considers the human person to be a complete person (Genesis 2:7; Numbers 23:10; Deuteronomy 6:5; 1 Thessalonians 5:23). This unity is severed only by death and then only temporarily until the natural, intended union is restored at the resurrection (2 Corinthians 5:8; 1 Thessalonians 4:13–17).

3. The Bible forbids murder because man is created in the image of God (Genesis 9:5, 6). The Bible further says that succeeding generations of men are conceived in the image of God (Genesis 5:1–3).

We call upon society and the church to show compassion toward unwed mothers and mothers of unwanted children. To this end, not only sympathetic counsel, but also concrete help should be extended (1 John 3:16–18; James 2:14–17).

But we also call upon our society to return to the law of God, recognizing the Word of God that "Righteousness exalts a nation, but sin is a reproach to any people (Proverbs 14:34).

17. Breck, 264.

Adopted by the 39th General Assembly of the Orthodox Presbyterian Church (Minutes, May 15–20, 1972, pp. 17–18, 149).[18]

PRESBYTERIAN CHURCH OF AMERICA

Conclusion

The fundamental task of the church is the proclamation of God's Word as it bears upon individuals and institutions. The Holy Scripture, which is God's Word written, is graciously given as the power of God unto salvation for those who believe. But it is no less the absolute authority given to regulate any institution or individual as regards the created life which only God has the right to give or take away. On this basis we believe the intentional killing of an unborn child is a violation of God's command and authority. Scripture considers such a child a person and thus covered by Divine protection even as a person after birth. Any medical support or historical precedent can only be of secondary authority when we have a clear Word from God on moral questions. Yet as often is the case, a candid evaluation of secondary authorities supports the teaching of Scripture. All truth is God's truth, and any alleged conflict is thus but a misreading of one area of His truth.

We are convinced Scripture forbids abortion. The premise of the personhood of the unborn child and the premise of the universal validity of the Sixth Commandment, if true, necessitates the conclusion that abortion is wrong. In a day in which situation ethics has left its mark, the question easily arises in the minds of some, "But what if?" The familiar objections are then presented: population control, economic hardships, unwanted children, psychological or physical health of the mother, rape or incest, deformed children, and protection for the mother's life. We have not dealt with these particular cases with the exception of where the mother's life is threatened. Neither have we dealt with frequently raised objections such as "freedom of choice" and dangers of illegal abortions. There are two primary reasons for not going into detail. One is practical. It would unnecessarily enlarge this report, and these objections have been adequately dealt with in the OPC and RPCES Reports and in other readily available sources. The other reason is to emphasize the principle set forth in this report. Abortion is wrong; it is sin. God as the righteous and holy Judge will not permit sin to be justified by human "situations." Thus the practical application in each of these cases is the consistent application of God's abso-

---

18. "Statement on Abortion from the 39th General Assembly 1972, Minutes, page 17–18, 149," from the Orthodox Presbyterian Church website. (Willow Grove, PA May 15–20, 1972 [cited 6 August 2007]); available from http://opc.org/GA/Abortion_GA39 .html; INTERNET.

lute prohibition and the comfort derived from the knowledge that our greatest good is dependent upon our obedience to God.

We cannot stress too strongly our authority in this matter. God in His Word speaks of the unborn child as a person and treats him as such, and so must we. The Bible teaches the sanctity of life, and so must we. The Bible, especially in the Sixth Commandment, gives concrete protection to that life which bears the image of God. We must uphold that commandment. There is a danger of weakening our witness by either retreating from an absolute ethic revealed in God's Word or by uncritically associating ourselves with a humanistic philosophy of right to life based on human wisdom. The Church as the repository of God's revelation must speak from that authority and must do so without compromise or equivocation.

> For Thou didst form my inward parts;
> Thou didst weave me in my mother's womb.
> I will give thanks to Thee, for I am fearfully
>   and wonderfully made
> Wonderful are Thy works,
> And my soul knows it very well.
>
> Search me, O God, and know my heart;
> Try me and know my anxious thoughts;
> And see if there be any hurtful way in me, and lead
>   me in the everlasting way. (Psalm 139:13, 14, 23, 24)[19]

PRESBYTERIAN CHURCH USA

Presbyterians have struggled with the issue of abortion for more than 30 years, beginning in 1970 when the General Assembly, the national governing body of the Presbyterian Church (U.S.A.) declared that, "the artificial or induced termination of a pregnancy is a matter of careful ethical decision of the patient . . . and therefore should not be restricted by law . . ." (1) In the years that followed this action, the General Assembly has adopted policy and taken positions on the subject of abortion.

In 2006 the 217th General Assembly approved language that clarified the Presbyterian Church (U.S.A.) position on problem pregnancies.

When an individual woman faces the decision whether to terminate a pregnancy, the issue is intensely personal, and may manifest itself in ways

---

19. "Report of the AD Interim Committee on Abortion at the 6th General Assembly 1978, Appendix O, page 270," from the PCA Historical Center website. (St. Louis, MO, 1978 [cited 28 June 2007]); available from http://www.pcahistory.org/pca/2-015.doc; INTERNET.

that do not reflect public rhetoric, or do not fit neatly into medical, legal, or policy guidelines. Humans are empowered by the spirit prayerfully to make significant moral choices, including the choice to continue or end a pregnancy. Human choices should not be made in a moral vacuum, but must be based on Scripture, faith, and Christian ethics. For any choice, we are accountable to God; however, even when we err, God offers to forgive us.(2)

The 217th General Assembly (2006) reiterated the role of the church in individual and families lives as they face problem pregnancy issues.

The church has a responsibility to provide public witness and to offer guidance, counsel, and support to those who make or interpret laws and public policies about abortion and problem pregnancies. Pastors have a duty to counsel with and pray for those who face decisions about problem pregnancies. Congregations have a duty to pray for and support those who face these choices, to offer support for women and families to help make unwanted pregnancies less likely to occur, and to provide practical support for those facing the birth of a child with medical anomalies, birth after rape or incest, or those who face health, economic, or other stresses.(3)

The church also affirms the value of children and the importance of nurturing, protecting, and advocating their well-being. The church, therefore, appreciates the challenge each woman and family face when issues of personal well-being arise in the later stages of a pregnancy.(4)

"In life and death, we belong to God." Life is a gift from God. We may not know exactly when human life begins, and have but an imperfect understanding of God as the giver of life and of our own human existence, yet we recognize that life is precious to God, and we should preserve and protect it. We derive our understanding of human life from Scripture and the Reformed Tradition in light of science, human experience, and reason guided by the Holy Spirit. Because we are made in the image of God, human beings are moral agents, endowed by the Creator with the capacity to make choices. Our Reformed Tradition recognizes that people do not always make moral choices, and forgiveness is central to our faith. In the Reformed Tradition, we affirm that God is the only Lord of conscience—not the state or the church. As a community, the church challenges the faithful to exercise their moral agency responsibly. (5) In regard to problems that arise in late pregnancies, the 217th General Assembly (2006) adopted the following position:

We affirm that the lives of viable unborn babies—those well-developed enough to survive outside the womb if delivered—ought to be preserved and cared for and not aborted. In cases where problems of life or health of the mother arise in a pregnancy, the church supports efforts to protect the life and health of both the mother and the baby. When late-term pregnancies must be terminated, we urge decisions intended to deliver the baby alive. We look to our churches to provide pastoral and tangible support to women in problem pregnancies and to surround these families with a community of care. We affirm adoption as a provision for women who deliver children they are not able to care for, and ask our churches to assist in seeking loving, Christian, adoptive families.(6)

This General Assembly holds this statement as its position on a Christian response to problems that arise late in pregnancies. We find it to be consistent with current General Assembly policy on Problem Pregnancies and Abortion (1992), and supersedes General Assembly statements of 2002 and 2003 on late-term pregnancies and abortion.(7)

The 204th General Assembly (1992) adopted the most comprehensive policy statement on pregnancy and abortion. The "Report of the Special Committee on Problem Pregnancy" addressed a myriad of issues in order to help guide individuals and families who face problem pregnancies and abortion. The following are excerpts from the 1992 policy:

"There is [both] agreement and disagreement on the basic issue of abortion. The committee [on problem pregnancies and abortion] agreed that there are no biblical texts that speak expressly to the topic of abortion, but that taken in their totality the Holy Scriptures are filled with messages that advocate respect for the woman and child before and after birth. Therefore the Presbyterian Church (U.S.A.) encourages an atmosphere of open debate and mutual respect for a variety of opinions concerning the issues related to problem pregnancies and abortion."(8)

Areas of Substantial Agreement on the Issue of Abortion

The church ought to be able to maintain within its fellowship those who, on the basis of a study of Scripture and prayerful decision, come to diverse conclusions and actions.

Problem pregnancies are the result of, and influenced by, so many complicated and insolvable circumstances that we have neither the wisdom nor the authority to address or decide each situation.

We affirm the ability and responsibility of women, guided by the Scriptures and the Holy Spirit, in the context of their communities of faith, to make good moral choices in regard to problem pregnancies.

We call upon Presbyterians to work for a decrease in the number of problem pregnancies, thereby decreasing the number of abortions.

The considered decision of a woman to terminate a pregnancy can be a morally acceptable, though certainly not the only or required, decision. Possible justifying circumstances would include medical indications of severe physical or mental deformity, conception as a result of rape or incest, or conditions under which the physical or mental health of either woman or child would be gravely threatened.

We are disturbed by abortions that seem to be elected only as a convenience or ease embarrassment. We affirm that abortion should not be used as a method of birth control.

Abortion is not morally acceptable for gender selection only or solely to obtain fetal parts for transplantation.

We reject the use of violence and/or abusive language either in protest of or in support of abortion . . .

The strong Christian presumption is that since all life is precious to God, we are to preserve and protect it. Abortion ought to be an option of last resort . . .

The Christian community must be concerned about and address the circumstances that bring a woman to consider abortion as the best available option. Poverty, unjust societal realities, sexism, racism, and inadequate supportive relationships may render a woman virtually powerless to choose freely.(9)

The previous except and the areas of substantial agreement on the issue of abortion have been the cornerstone for "the atmosphere of open debate and mutual respect for a variety of opinions" over the past 30 years.

1) Minutes of the 182nd General Assembly (1970), Presbyterian Church (U.S.A.), p. 891

2) Minutes of the 217th General Assembly (2006), Presbyterian Church (U.S.A.), p. 905

3) Minutes of the 217th General Assembly (2006), Presbyterian Church (U.S.A.), p. 905

4) Minutes of the 217th General Assembly (2006), Presbyterian Church (U.S.A.), p. 905

5) Minutes of the 217th General Assembly (2006), Presbyterian Church (U.S.A.), p. 905

6) Minutes of the 217th General Assembly (2006), Presbyterian Church (U.S.A.), p. 905

7) Minutes of the 217th General Assembly (2006), Presbyterian Church (U.S.A.), p. 905

8) Minutes of the 204th General Assembly (1992), Presbyterian Church (U.S.A.), p. 367–368, 372–374

9) Minutes of the 204th General Assembly (1992), Presbyterian Church (U.S.A.), p. 367–368, 372–374 [20]

SOUTHERN BAPTIST CONVENTION

Resolution #8: On Thirty Years of Roe V. Wade, adopted at the SBC convention, June 2003:

WHEREAS, Scripture reveals that all human life is created in the image of God, and therefore sacred to our Creator (Genesis 1:27; Genesis 9:6); and

20. "Presbyterian 101:Abortion Issues," from the Presbyterian Church USA website. (Louisville, KY [cited 27 June 2007]); available from http://www.pcusa.org/101/index.htm; INTERNET.

WHEREAS, The Bible affirms that the unborn baby is a person bearing the image of God from the moment of conception (Psalm 139:13–16; Luke 1:44); and

WHEREAS, Scripture further commands the people of God to plead for protection for the innocent and justice for the fatherless (Psalm 72:12–14; Psalm 82:3; James 1:27); and

WHEREAS, January 2003 marked thirty years since the 1973 United States Supreme Court Roe v. Wade decision, which legalized abortion in all fifty states; and

WHEREAS, Resolutions passed by the Southern Baptist Convention in 1971 and 1974 accepted unbiblical premises of the abortion rights movement, forfeiting the opportunity to advocate the protection of defenseless women and children; and

WHEREAS, During the early years of the post-Roe era, some of those then in leadership positions within the denomination endorsed and furthered the "pro-choice" abortion rights agenda outlined in Roe v. Wade; and

WHEREAS, Some political leaders have referenced 1970s-era Southern Baptist Convention resolutions and statements by former Southern Baptist Convention leaders to oppose legislative efforts to protect women and children from abortion; and

WHEREAS, Southern Baptist churches have effected a renewal of biblical orthodoxy and confessional integrity in our denomination, beginning with the Southern Baptist Convention presidential election of 1979; and

WHEREAS, The Southern Baptist Convention has maintained a robust commitment to the sanctity of all human life, including that of the unborn, beginning with a landmark pro-life resolution in 1982; and

WHEREAS, Our confessional statement, The Baptist Faith and Message, affirms that children "from the moment of conception, are a blessing and heritage from the Lord"; and further affirms that Southern Baptists are mandated by Scripture to speak on behalf of the unborn and contend for the sanctity of all human life from conception to natural death; and

WHEREAS, The legacy of Roe v. Wade has grown to include ongoing assaults on human life such as euthanasia, the harvesting of human embryos for the purposes of medical experimentation, and an accelerating move toward human cloning; now, therefore, be it

RESOLVED, That the messengers to the Southern Baptist Convention meeting in Phoenix, Arizona, June 17–18, 2003, reiterate our conviction that the 1973 Roe v. Wade decision was based on a fundamentally flawed understanding of the United States Constitution, human embryology, and the basic principles of human rights; and be it further

RESOLVED, That we reaffirm our belief that the Roe v. Wade decision was an act of injustice against innocent unborn children as well as against vulnerable women in crisis pregnancy situations, both of which have been victimized by a "sexual revolution" that empowers predatory and irresponsible men and by a lucrative abortion industry that has fought against even the most minimal restrictions on abortion; and be it further

RESOLVED, That we offer our prayers, our love, and our advocacy for women and men who have been abused by abortion and the emotional, spiritual, and physical aftermath of this horrific practice; affirming that the gospel of Jesus Christ grants complete forgiveness for any sin, including that of abortion; and be it further

RESOLVED, That we lament and renounce statements and actions by previous Conventions and previous denominational leadership that offered support to the abortion culture; and be it further

RESOLVED, That we humbly confess that the initial blindness of many in our Convention to the enormity of Roe v. Wade should serve as a warning to contemporary Southern Baptists of the subtlety of the spirit of the age in obscuring a biblical worldview; and be it further

RESOLVED, That we urge our Southern Baptist churches to remain vigilant in the protection of human life by preaching the whole counsel of God on matters of human sexuality and the sanctity of life, by encouraging and empowering Southern Baptists to adopt unwanted children, by providing spiritual, emotional, and financial support for women in crisis pregnancies, and by calling on our government officials to take action to protect the lives of women and children; and be it further

RESOLVED, That we express our appreciation to both houses of Congress for their passage of the Partial-Birth Abortion Ban Act of 2003, and we applaud President Bush for his commitment to sign this bill into law; and be it further

RESOLVED, That we urge Congress to act swiftly to deliver this bill to President Bush for his signature; and be it finally

RESOLVED, That we pray and work for the repeal of the Roe v. Wade decision and for the day when the act of abortion will be not only illegal, but also unthinkable. Phoenix.[21]

21. "Southern Baptist Convention Resolutions on Abortion: Resolution #8: On Thirty Years of Roe v. Wade, adopted at the SBC convention, June 2003," from the Southern Baptist Convention website. (Nashville, TN, 2003 [cited 17 January 2008]); available

UNITED CHURCH OF CHRIST
Reproductive Rights

> But Jesus said, "Someone touched me; for I noticed that power had gone out from me." (Luke 8:46)

God has given us life, and life is sacred and good. God has also given us the responsibility to make decisions which reflect a reverence for life in circumstances when conflicting realities are present. Jesus affirmed women as full partners in the faith, capable of making decisions that affect their lives.

If the full range of options available to women concerning reproductive health are compromised, then women's moral agency and ability to make decisions consistent with their faith are compromised. Furthermore, poor women should have equal access to full reproductive health services, including abortion and information on family planning.

The United Church of Christ has affirmed and re-affirmed since 1971 that access to safe and legal abortion is consistent with a woman's right to follow the dictates of her own faith and beliefs in determining when and if she should have children, and has supported comprehensive sexuality education as one measure to prevent unwanted or unplanned pregnancies (General Synods VIII, IX, XI, XII, XIII, XVI, XVII, and XVIII).[22]

UNITED METHODIST CHURCH

The beginning of life and the ending of life are the God-given boundaries of human existence. While individuals have always had some degree of control over when they would die, they now have the awesome power to determine when and even whether new individuals will be born.

Our belief in the sanctity of unborn human life makes us reluctant to approve abortion. But we are equally bound to respect the sacredness of the life and well-being of the mother, for whom devastating damage may result from an unacceptable pregnancy. In continuity with past Christian teaching, we recognize tragic conflicts of life with life that may justify abortion, and in such cases we support the legal option of abortion under proper medical procedures. We cannot affirm abortion as an acceptable means of birth control, and we unconditionally reject it as a means of gender selection.

---

from http://www.sbc.net/resolutions/amResolution.asp?ID=1130; INTERNET.

22. "Reproductive Rights," from the United Church of Christ website. (Cleveland, OH, 2004 [cited 20 June 2007]); available from http://www.ucc.org/justice/choice/; INTERNET.

We oppose the use of late-term abortion known as dilation and extraction (partial-birth abortion) and call for the end of this practice except when the physical life of the mother is in danger and no other medical procedure is available, or in the case of severe fetal anomalies incompatible with life. We call all Christians to a searching and prayerful inquiry into the sorts of conditions that may warrant abortion. We commit our Church to continue to provide nurturing ministries to those who terminate a pregnancy, to those in the midst of a crisis pregnancy, and to those who give birth. We particularly encourage the Church, the government, and social service agencies to support and facilitate the option of adoption. (See ¶ 161.K.)

Governmental laws and regulations do not provide all the guidance required by the informed Christian conscience. Therefore, a decision concerning abortion should be made only after thoughtful and prayerful consideration by the parties involved, with medical, pastoral, and other appropriate counsel.[23]

WESLEYAN CHURCH

Abortion. The Wesleyan Church seeks to recognize and preserve the sanctity of human life from conception to natural death and, thus, is opposed to the use of induced abortion. However, it recognizes that there may be rare pregnancies where there are grave medical conditions threatening the life of the mother, which could raise a serious question about taking the life of the unborn child. In such a case, a decision should be made only after very prayerful consideration following medical and spiritual counseling. The Wesleyan Church encourages its members to become informed about the abortion issue and to become actively involved locally and nationally in the preparation and passage of appropriate legislation guaranteeing protection of life under law to unborn children.[24]

23. "Social Principles: Abortion," from the *Book of Discipline of the United Methodist Church* in the United Methodist Church website. (Nashville, TN: United Methodist Publishing House, 2004 [cited 26 June 2007]); available from http://archives.umc.org/ interior.asp?mid=1732; INTERNET.

24. *The Discipline of the Wesleyan Church 2004*, 42.

Appendix II

Member Organizations of the National Pro-Life Religious Council

ALPHA OMEGA LIFE, INC.
Vera Faith Lord
(410) 948-8070
alphaomegalife@verizon.net

ANGLICANS FOR LIFE
Georgette Forney, President, Anglicans for Life
Co-founder, Silent No More Awareness Campaign
405 Frederick Avenue
Sewickley, PA 15143
(412)749-0455
(800)707-6635
Georgette@AnglicansforLife.org
www.AnglicansforLife.org
www.SilentNoMoreAwareness.org

CEC FOR LIFE
Canon Terry Gensemer
(205) 786-2805 x4
cecforlife@aol.com

COMMON GOOD
Randolph Sly
(703) 404-0754
rws@slynet.org

CONSERVATIVE CONGREGATIONAL
CHRISTIAN CONFERENCE
Jan Kirk van der Swaagh (Vice President of the NPRC)
8941 Highway 5, Lake Elmo, MN 55042
(651) 739-1474
jkvanderswaagh@ccccusa.com

LIFE EDUCATION AND RESOURCE NETWORK (LEARN)
Rev. Dr. Clenard H. Childress, Jr.
P.O. Box 157, Montclair, NJ 07042
(866) 242-4997
prophetcleo@aol.com

LUTHERAN CHURCH-MISSOURI SYNOD (LCMS)
Maggie Karner
Ed Szeto
1333 S Kirkwood St, Saint Louis, MO 63122
(800) 248-1930 ext. 1380
(765) 289-0180
maggie.karner@lcms.org

LUTHERANS FOR LIFE
Dennis Di Mauro (Secretary of the NPRC)
1120 South G Avenue, Nevada, IA 50201-2774
1-888-364-LIFE
dennisdimauro@yahoo.com

NATIONAL BLACK PRO-LIFE UNION
Day Gardner
P.O. Box 76452, Washington, DC 20013
(202) 834-0844
dgardner@NBPLU.com

NATIONAL CLERGY COUNCIL AND NATIONAL
PRO-LIFE ACTION CENTER
Rev. Rob Schenck and Dr. Paul Schenck
109 2nd Street, NE
Washington, DC 20002
(202) 546-8329
www.nplac.org

NATIONAL RIGHT TO LIFE COMMITTEE,
RELIGIOUS OUTREACH
Ernest Ohlhoff (Treasurer of the NPRC)
512 10th St., NW, Washington, DC 20004
(202) 626-8811
Ernie@nrlc.org

PRESBYTERIANS PRO-LIFE
Marie Bowen, Executive Director
3942 Middle Rd., Allison Park, PA 15101
(412) 487-1990
ppl@ppl.org

PRIESTS FOR LIFE
Father Frank Pavone (President of the NPRC)
P.O. Box 141172, Staten Island, NY 10314
(718) 980-4400
mail@priestsforlife.org

TASKFORCE OF UNITED METHODISTS ON ABORTION
AND SEXUALITY/LIFEWATCH
Rev. Paul T. Stallsworth
(252) 726-2175
stpeters@mail.clis.com

UNITED CHURCH OF CHRIST FRIENDS FOR LIFE
John B. Brown, Jr.
(610) 754-6446
SothJBrown1@aol.com

Interested Parties in NPRC

Pamela Brozowski
Outreach Assistant
National Right to Life
(202) 378-8855
(202) 393-2610
pbrozowski@nrlc.org

Bishop Craig Bates
Charismatic Episcopal Church
995 Oceanfront
Long Beach, NY 11561
(516) 599-3780
InterNY@aol.com

Janet Morana
Priests for Life
P.O. Box 141172
Staten Island, NY 10314
(718) 980-4400 ext. 246
janet@priestsforlife.org

Kathleen Sweeney
NPRC Newsletter
kathleen_sweeney@comcast.net

Tom Grenchik
Director of the Pro-Life Office for
the Archdiocese of Washington
3211 4th St., NE
Washington, DC 20017-1194
(202) 541-3000
prolife@usccb.org

Bibliography

"Abortion," by the Department for Studies, Division for Church in Society from the Evangelical Lutheran Church of America website. Chicago, IL, Sept. 1991 [cited 27 June 2007]; available from http://www.elca.org/SocialStatements/abortion/; INTERNET.

"Abortion Foe Speaks to Clinton," *St. Paul Pioneer Press (MN)*, December 27, 1996, 4A.

"American Baptist Church Resolution Concerning Abortion and Ministry in the Local Church," in *The Abortion Debate in the United States and Canada: A Source Book*. Muldoon, Maureen, ed., 69–74. New York: Garland Publishing Inc., 1991.

Armstrong, James. "Word of Hope," in *Prayerfully Pro-Choice: Resources for Worship*, 38–40, Washington, D.C.: Religious Coalition for Reproductive Choice, 2000.

Barrett, David B., et. al. *World Christian Encyclopedia*, vol. 1, 2nd ed. New York: Oxford University Press, 2001.

Barry, Robert L. *The Sanctity of Human Life and Its Protection*. Lanham, MD: University Press of America, 2002.

Barth, Karl. *Church Dogmatics*, vol. 4, part 4. Edinburgh: T & T Clark, 1961.

St. Basil, "First Canonical Epistle to Amphilochius," in *The Early Church Fathers on CD-ROM*. Salem, OR: Harmony Media Inc., 2000.

Beisel, Nicola. *Imperiled Innocents: Anthony Comstock and Family Reproduction in Victorian America*. Princeton: Princeton University Press, 1997.

"Beliefs: Abortion," from the Assemblies of God website. Springfield, MO, 1985 [cited 3 July 2007]; available from http://ag.org/top/Beliefs/contempissues_01_abortion.cfm; INTERNET.

Bonhoeffer, Dietrich. *Ethics*. New York: Touchstone, 1955.

Bonner, G. "Abortion and Early Christian Thought." in *Abortion and the Sanctity of Human Life*, ed. by J. H. Channer, 93-122. Exeter, UK: Paternoster Ltd., 1985.

Bowen, Marie. E-mail interview by author, August 8, 2007.

Breck, John. *The Sacred Gift of Life: Orthodox Christianity and Bioethics*. Crestwood, NY: St. Vladimir's Press. 1998.

"Brief History of Lutherans For Life," in Lutherans For Life website. Nevada, IA, 2007 [cited 11 June 2007]; available from http://www.lutheransforlife.org/Who_Are_We/brief_history.htm; INTERNET.

Brodie, Janet Farrell. *Contraception and Abortion in Nineteenth Century America*. Ithaca, NY: Cornell University Press, 1994.

Brown, Harold O. J. *Death Before Birth*. New York: Thomas Nelson Inc. Publishers, 1977.

Bibliography

Brown, John B. "Rejoicing in the Truth," in *The Right Choice*, ed. by Paul T. Stallsworth, 35–42, Nashville, TN: Abingdon Press, 1997.

————. Telephone interview by the author, Sept 10, 2007.

————, and Robin Fox, eds. *Affirming Life: Biblical Perspectives on Abortion for the United Church of Christ.* Princeton, NJ: Princeton University Press, 1991.

"The Canons of the Council of Ancyra," in *The Early Church Fathers on CD-ROM.* Salem OR: Harmony Media Inc., 2000.

"The Canons of the Council in Trullo," in *The Early Church Fathers on CD-ROM.* Salem OR: Harmony Media Inc., 2000.

Catechism of the Catholic Church. New Hope, KY: Urbi et Orbi Communications, 1994.

"CCCC Position Papers: Statement On Abortion," from the Conservative Congregational Christian Conference website. Lake Elmo, MN [cited 27 June 2007]; available from http://www.ccccusa.com/files/CCCCPositionPapers.pdf; INTERNET.

Channer, J. H., ed., *Abortion and the Sanctity of Human Life.* Exeter, UK: Paternoster Press Ltd., 1985.

"Le Christianisme dans le monde," *Le Point.* Hors-série, no. 11, Novembre–Décembre 2006, 10-11.

"Coalition President" in Religious Coalition for Reproductive Choice website. Washington, D.C. July 2006 [cited 24 August 2007]; available from http://www.rcrc.org/about/president.cfm; INTERNET.

Connery, John. *Abortion: The Development of the Roman Catholic Perspective.* New Orleans, LA: Loyola University Press, 1977.

"Constitutions of the Holy Apostles," in *The Early Church Fathers on CD-ROM.* Salem, OR: Harmony Media Inc., 2000.

Conway, William, et. al., *Human Life is Sacred.* Dublin: Veritas Publications, 1975.

Davis, Tom. *Sacred Work.* New Brunswick, NJ: Rutgers University Press, 2005.

"Day Gardner," from the National Pro-Life Action Center web page. Washington, D.C. [cited 27 December 2007] available from http://www.nplac.org/bios/bio-dgardner.html; INTERNET.

Desteffano, Anthony. "How Did Priests for Life Start?" *Priests for Life Newsletter.* Volume 11, Number 1, January–February 2001, 1–2.

"Didache," in *Lost Scriptures: Books that Did Not Make It into the New Testament,* ed. by Bart D. Ehrman, 211–17. New York: Oxford University Press, 2003.

Dillon, Michele. "The Abortion Debate: Good for the Church and Good for American Society," in *American Catholics, American Culture, Traditions and Resistance,* ed. by Margaret O'Brien Steinfels, 71–75. New York: Rowman and Littlefield, 2004.

The Discipline of the Wesleyan Church 2004. Indianapolis, IN: Wesleyan Publishing House, 2005.

Dobson, James. Interview with the author, Nov. 29, 2007.

Doerflinger, Richard M. "The Pro-Life Message and Catholic Social Teaching: Problems of Reception," in *American Catholics, American Culture, Traditions and Resistance,* ed. by Margaret O'Brien Steinfels, 49–58, New York: Rowman and Littlefield, 2004.

Dombrowski, Daniel M. and Robert J. Deltete, *A Brief, Liberal, Catholic Defense of Abortion.* Urbanna, IL: University of Illinois Press, 2000.

"The Epistle of Barnabas," in *The Early Church Fathers on CD-ROM.* Salem OR: Harmony Media Inc., 2000.

Bibliography

"Father Frank A. Pavone—Biography," in Priests for Life website. Staten Island, NY, 2007 [cited 3 July 2007]; available from http://www.priestsforlife.org/intro/ffbio.html; INTERNET.

Ficarra, Bernard J. *Abortion Analyzed*. Old Town, ME: Health Educator Publications, Inc., 1989.

Forney, Georgette. E-mail interview by the author, October 5, 2007.

Franks, Angela. *Margaret Sanger's Eugenic Legacy: The Control of Female Fertility*. Jefferson, NC: McFarland and Co., 2005.

"Frequently Asked Questions>Moral and Ethical Issues>Life Issues>Abortion," from the Lutheran Church—Missouri Synod website. St. Louis, MO, 2003–2007 [cited 27 June 2007]; available from http://www.lcms.org/pages/internal.asp?NavID=2120; INTERNET.

Gardner, Day. E-mail interview with the author, December 23, 2007.

Garton, Jean. E-mail interview with the author, November 10–13, 2007.

———. "Where are the Shepherds?" in *Back to the Drawing Board: The Future of the Pro-Life Movement*, ed. by Teresa R. Wagner, 229–237. South Bend, IN: St. Augustine's Press, 2003.

———. *Who Broke the Baby? What The Abortion Slogans Really Mean*. Minneapolis, MN: Bethany House, 1998.

"General Assembly Resolution NO. 0725 (Sense-of-the-Assembly) Proactive Prevention: Seeking Common Ground on the Issue of Abortion," from the Christian Church—Disciples of Christ website. Indianapolis, IN, 2007 [cited 15 August 2007]; available from http://www.disciples.org/ga/resolutions/0725/; INTERNET.

General Convention, *Journal of the General Convention of the Protestant Episcopal Church, 1967*. New York: Protestant Episcopal Press, 1968.

General Convention, *Journal of the General Convention of the Protestant Episcopal Church, 1976*. New York: Protestant Episcopal Press, 1977.

General Convention, *Journal of the General Convention of the Protestant Episcopal Church, 1982*. New York: Protestant Episcopal Press, 1983.

General Convention, *Journal of the General Convention of the Protestant Episcopal Church, Phoenix 1991*. New York: Domestic and Foreign Missionary Society of the Protestant Episcopal Church in the USA, 1992.

General Convention, *Journal of the General Convention of the Protestant Episcopal Church, 1994*. New York: Domestic and Foreign Missionary Society of the Protestant Episcopal Church in the USA, 1995.

Gensemer, Terry. Telephone interview by author, July 30, 2007.

Gibbons, Kendyl. "Ceremony for Closure after an Abortion," in *Prayerfully Pro-Choice: Resources for Worship*, 85–88. Washington, D.C.: Religious Coalition for Reproductive Choice, 2000.

Gorman, Michael J. *Abortion and the Early Church*. Eugene OR: Wipf and Stock Publishers, 1998.

———. "Ahead to Our Past: Abortion and Christian Texts," in *The Church and Abortion*, ed. by Paul T. Stallsworth, 25–43. Nashville: Abingdon Press, 1993.

———. E-mail interview with the author, August 12, 2007 and January 2, 2008.

———, and Ann Loar Brooks. *Holy Abortion?* Eugene OR: Wipf and Stock Publishers, 2003.

———. "Why Is the New Testament Silent About Abortion?" *Christianity Today*. January 11, 1993, 27–29.

Gorney, Cynthia. *Articles of Faith: A Frontline History of the Abortion Wars.* New York: Simon and Schuster, 1998.

"Greek Orthodox Archdiocese of North and South America: A Statement on Abortion," in *The Abortion Debate in the United States and Canada: A Source Book,* ed. by Maureen Muldoon, 86–87. New York: Garland Publishing Inc., 1991.

Grube, George W., ed. *What the Church Fathers Say About . . . ,* vols. 1 and 2. Minneapolis, MN: Light and Life Publishing Co., 2005.

Hauerwas, Stanley. "Abortion Theologically Understood," in *The Church and Abortion,* ed. by Paul T. Stallsworth, 44–66. Nashville: Abingdon Press, 1993.

Hayes, Richard B. *The Moral Vision of the New Testament: Community, Cross, New Creation.* San Francisco: Harper Collins Publishers, 1996.

Hendershott, Anne. *The Politics of Abortion.* New York: Encounter Books, 2006.

"History and Overview of Anglicans for Life," in Anglicans for Life website. Sewickley, PA, 2007 [cited 25 June 2007]; available from http://www.anglicansforlife.org/about/history.asp; INTERNET.

"History of Concerned Women for America" from the Concerned Woman for America website. Washington, D.C. [cited 7 January 2008]; available from http://www.cwfa.org/history.asp; INTERNET.

"HR 1833 and the United Church of Christ," in the Worldwide faith News website. New York: 20 May 1996 [cited 31 December 2007]; available from http://www.wfn.org/1996/05/msg00749.html; INTERNET.

Hunter, Johnny. Telephone interview with the author, December 27, 2007.

Jacoby, Kerry N. *Souls, Bodies, Spirits.* Westport, CT: Praeger Publishers, 1998.

Joffe, C. et al., "The Crisis of Abortion Provision and Pro-Choice Medical Activism in the 1990's," in *Abortion Wars: A Half Century of Struggle 1950–2000,* ed. by Rickie Solinger, 320-333. Berkeley: University of California Press, 1998.

John Chrysostom, "Commentary on the Epistle of St. Paul to the Romans," in *The Early Church Fathers on CD-ROM.* Salem OR: Harmony Media Inc. 2000.

John Paul II. *The Gospel of Life.* New York: Random House, 1995.

———, *The Theology of the Body: Human Love in the Divine Plan.* Boston. MA: Pauline Books and Media, 1997.

Jones, Charles and Terry Gensemer, "A Declaration on the Sanctity of Human Life," from The International Communion of the Charismatic Episcopal Church website. San Clemente, CA, February 27, 2002 [cited 27 June 2007]; available from http://www.iccec.org/iccecnews/houseof_bishops/declarations/sanctityhumanlife_feb2002.html; INTERNET.

Kapparis, Konstantinos. *Abortion in the Ancient World.* London: Gerald Duckworth and Co. Ltd., 2002.

King, Alveda C. "Dr. Alveda C. King," from the King for America website. Atlanta, GA [cited 18 December 2007] available from http://www.kingforamerica.com/adkfoundation_article2.htm; INTERNET.

Klotz, John W. *A Christian View of Abortion.* St. Louis, MO: Concordia Publishing House, 1973.

Koop, C. Everett MD and Francis A. Schaeffer, *Whatever Happened to the Human Race?* Westchester, Ill.: Crossway Books, 1979.

Lamb, James. E-mail interview with the author, September 19, 2007.

———, gen. ed. *God's Word for Life.* Orange Park, FL: God's Word to the Nations, 2005.

"Landmarks in UCC Renewal," *The Witness,* Winter 2004, 16.

"Largest Religious Bodies," from the Adherents.com website. 18 May 2007 [accessed 5 September, 2007] available from http://www.adherents.com/adh_rb.html# International; INTERNET.

Lord, Vera Faith. E-mail interview by the author, July 30, 2007.

Luther, Martin. *Luther's Works* vol. 26, ed. by Jaroslav Pelikan and Helmut Lehmann. St. Louis: Concordia Publishing, 1964.

Luthringer, George. *Considering Abortion? Clarifying What You Believe*. Washington, D.C.: Religious Coalition for Reproductive Choice, 1992.

Maguire, Daniel C. *Sacred Choices: the Right to Contraception and Abortion in Ten World Religions*. Minneapolis, MN: Fortress Press, 2001.

"'A Major Step Forward in Unity' In Reformed Family Of Churches," from World Alliance of Reformed Churches website. Geneva, January 2, 2006 [accessed 6 September, 2007] available from http://warc.jalb.de/warcajsp/side.jsp?news_id=631&part_id=0&navi=6; INTERNET.

Manual of the Church of the Nazarene 2005–2009. Kansas City, MO: Nazarene Publishing House, 2005.

Marx, Paul. *Death Peddlars: War on the Unborn*. Collegeville, MN: St. John's University Press, 1971.

McGreevy, John T. *Catholicism and American Freedom*. New York: W.W. Norton and Co., 2003.

———. "Catholics in America: Antipathy and Assimilation," in *American Catholics, American Culture, Traditions and Resistance*, ed. by Margaret O'Brien Steinfels, 3–26. New York: Rowman and Littlefield, 2004.

Minucius Felix. "The Octavius," in *The Early Church Fathers on CD-ROM*. Salem OR: Harmony Media Inc., 2000.

Mohr, James C. *Abortion in America: The Origins and Evolution of National Policy, 1800–1900*. New York: Oxford University Press, 1978.

"Moral Standards: Abortion," from the Evangelical Congregational Church website. Myerstown, PA [cited 27 June 2007] available from http://www.eccenter.com/files/ecc/publications/discipline/moral_standards.pdf; INTERNET.

Mother Teresa of Calcutta, "Whatever You Did unto One of the Least, You Did unto Me," in *The Right Choice*, ed. by Paul T. Stallsworth, 101–10. Nashville, TN: Abingdon Press, 1997.

Neu, Diann. "Affirming a Choice," in *Prayerfully Pro-Choice: Resources for Worship*, 82–84. Washington, D.C.: Religious Coalition for Reproductive Choice, 2000.

———. "You Are Not Alone: Seeking Wisdom to Decide," in *Prayerfully Pro-Choice: Resources for Worship*, 80–81, Washington, D.C.: Religious Coalition for Reproductive Choice, 2000.

Neuhaus, Richard John. "Abortion: The Dangerous Assumptions," *Commonweal*. 30 June 1967, 408–13.

———. "The Religion of the Sovereign Self," in *The Right Choice*, ed. by Paul T. Stallsworth, 61–68, Nashville, TN: Abingdon Press, 1997.

———. Telephone and e-mail interview with the author, September 11 and 13, 2007.

"News Archives: Abortion," in the United Methodist Church website. Nashville, TN, June 1, 2001 [cited 26 June 2007]; available from http://archives.umc.org/umns/backgrounders.asp?ptid=2&story={FB3D4877-CA2B-4BBE-B0A6-B74DAB578 C6F}&mid=905; INTERNET.

Bibliography

Nicholson, Susan T. *Abortion and the Roman Catholic Church*. Notre Dame, IN: Religious Ethics, Inc., 1978.

"Ninth All American Council of the Orthodox Church in America, Sept 19–24, 1989, General Statement," in *The Abortion Debate in the United States and Canada: A Source Book*, Muldoon, Maureen, ed., 89–90. New York: Garland Publishing Inc., 1991.

Noonan, John T. Jr., ed. *The Morality of Abortion: Legal and Historical Perspectives*. Cambridge, MA: Harvard University Press, 1970.

"Number of Lutherans Worldwide Increases to Nearly 64 Million," from the Lutheran World Federation web site. Geneva, 24 January 2001, Lutheran World Information [cited 5 September, 2007] available from http://www.lutheranworld.org/News/LWI/EN/231.EN.html; INTERNET.

O'Connor, John Cardinal "Commemoration of the Twentieth Anniversary of *Roe vs. Wade*," in *The Right Choice*, ed. by Paul T. Stallsworth, 69–76, Nashville, TN: Abingdon Press, 1997.

"On Abortion," from Position Papers and Pastoral Letters on the Evangelical Presbyterian Church website. June 1996 [cited 2 August 2007]; available from http://www.epc.org/about-epc/position-papers/abortion.html; INTERNET.

"Origin and History of LIFEWATCH," in the Lifewatch website. Cottleville, MO [cited 26 June 2007]; available from http://lifewatch.org/origin_and_history_of_lifewatch.html; INTERNET.

Otto, Randall E. "The Relativism of Pro-Choice Ethics," in *Affirming Life: Biblical Perspectives on Abortion for the United Church of Christ*, ed. by John B. Brown Jr. and Robin Fox, 2–11. Princeton, NJ: Princeton University Press, 1991.

"Our Founder—The Rev. Paul Marx, OSB" in Human Life International website. Front Royal, VA, October 12, 2002 [cited 24 August 2007]; available from http://www.hli.org/rev_paul_marx_tribute.html; INTERNET.

Parker, Joseph. Telephone interview by author, August 27, 2007.

Pavone, Frank. E-mail interview with the author, September 22, 2007.

———. *Ending Abortion, Not Just Fighting It*. Totowa, NJ: Catholic Book Publishing Company, 2006.

"Pentecostals," from the biblia.com website. April 2006 [accessed 5 September 2007] available from http://biblia.com/christianity2/3b-pentecostals.htm; INTERNET.

Petersen, William. *From Persons to People*. New Brunswick, NJ: Transaction Publishers, 2003.

Prayerfully Pro-Choice: Resources for Worship. Washington, D.C.: Religious Coalition for Reproductive Choice, 2000.

"Presbyterian 101: Abortion Issues," from the Presbyterian Church USA website. Louisville, KY [cited 27 June 2007]; available from http://www.pcusa.org/101/index.htm; INTERNET.

Presbyterian Social Witness Policy Compilation. Louisville, KY: Advisory Committee on Social Witness Policy of the General Assembly Council, Presbyterian Church (U.S.A.), 2000.

Presbyterian Social Witness Policy Compilation. in the Presbyterian Church, USA website. Louisville, KY: Advisory Committee on Social Witness Policy of the General Assembly Council, Presbyterian Church (U.S.A.), 2007 [cited 29 August 2007] available from http://index.pcusa.org/NXT/gateway.dll/socialpolicy/chapter00000.htm? fn=default.htm$f=templates$3.0; INTERNET.

Protopapas, John. E-mail interview by the author, August 12, 2007.

Bibliography

Purdue, Joretta. "United Methodists agreed more on abortion issue 25 years ago," Washington, D.C., United Methodist News Service (Release #35) (10-21-71B)562, January 21, 1998 [cited 26 June 2007]; available from http://dev.umns.umc.org/98/jan/35.htm; INTERNET.

Ragsdale, Katherine Hancock. "Faithful Witness for Choice," in *Prayerfully Pro-Choice: Resources for Worship*, 27–31. Washington, D.C.: Religious Coalition for Reproductive Choice, 2000.

"Report of the AD Interim Committee on Abortion at the 6th General Assembly 1978, Appendix O, page 270," from the PCA Historical Center website. St. Louis, MO, 1978 [cited 28 June 2007]; available from http://www.pcahistory.org/pca/2-015.doc; INTERNET.

"Reproductive Rights," from the United Church of Christ website. Cleveland, OH, 2004 [cited 20 June 2007]; available from http://www.ucc.org/justice/choice/; INTERNET.

"Resolution Number 1994-A054," General Convention, *Journal of the General Convention of . . . The Episcopal Church, Indianapolis,* 1994. New York: General Convention, 1995.

"Resolutions/Abortion," from the Moravian Church -Northern Province website. Bethlehem, PA, 2000 [cited 15 Aug. 2007]; available from http://www.mcnp.org/Documents/Resolutions/Abortion.asp; INTERNET.

"Resolutions on the Sanctity of Human Life by Pro-Life Lutheran Bodies," in Lutherans for Life website. Nevada, IA, 2007 [cited 11 June 2007]; available from www.lutheransforlife.org/PDF_Files/Resolutions_-_Lutheran_Church_Bodies.pdf; INTERNET.

Riddle, John M. *Contraception and Abortion for the Ancient World to the Renaissance.* Cambridge, MA: Harvard University Press, 1992.

————. *Eve's Herbs.* Cambridge, MA: Harvard University Press, 1998.

Risen, James and Judy Thomas, *Wrath of Angels: The American Abortion War.* New York: Basic Books, 1998.

Robinson, Luke J. Interview with the author, December 20, 2007, Frederick, MD.

Rogerson, J. W. "Using the Bible in the Debate About Abortion." in *Abortion and the Sanctity of Human Life*, ed. by J. H. Channer, 77–92. Exeter, UK: Paternoster Ltd., 1985.

Ross, Loretta J. "African American Women," in *Abortion Wars: A Half Century of Struggle 1950–2000*, ed. by Rickie Solinger, 161-207. Berkeley: University of California Press, 1998.

Rubin, Eva R. ed., *The Abortion Controversy: A Documentary History.* Westport CT: Greenwood Press, 1994.

Schenck, Rob. Telephone interview with the author, January 3, 2008.

Schmidt, Alvin. *Under the Influence.* Grand Rapids, MI: Zondervan Publishing House, 2001.

Sheldon, Ben. Telephone interview by author, August 24, 2007.

Signer, Marjorie and Cynthia Cooper, "Six Billion People—A Matter of Consequence," in *Prayerfully Pro-Choice: Resources for Worship*, 97–99. Washington, D.C.: Religious Coalition for Reproductive Choice, 2000.

Simmons, Paul D. "Some Biblical References to Personhood," in *Prayerfully Pro-Choice: Resources for Worship*, 116–18. Washington, D.C.: Religious Coalition for Reproductive Choice, 2000.

"Social Principles: Abortion," from the Book of Discipline of the United Methodist Church in the United Methodist Church website. Nashville, TN: United Methodist Publishing House, 2004 [cited 26 June 2007]; available from http://archives.umc.org/interior.asp?mid=1732; INTERNET.

Bibliography

"Social Statement on Abortion," in Evangelical Lutheran Church of America website. Chicago, IL, 2007 [cited 21 June 2007]; available from http://www.elca.org/SocialStatements/abortion; INTERNET.

Solinger, Rickie, ed. *Abortion Wars: A Half Century of Struggle* 1950–2000. Berkeley: University of California Press, 1998.

Soper, J. Christopher. *Evangelical Christianity in the United States and Great Britain.* New York: New York University Press, 1994.

"Southern Baptist Convention Resolutions on Abortion: Resolution #8: On Thirty Years of Roe v. Wade, adopted at the SBC convention, June 2003," from the Southern Baptist Convention website. Nashville, TN: 2003 [cited 17 January 2008]; available from http://www.sbc.net/resolutions/amResolution.asp?ID=1130; INTERNET.

Sproul, R. C. *Abortion: A Rational Look at an Emotional Issue.* Colorado Springs, CO: NavPress, 1990.

Stallsworth, Paul T. ed., *The Church and Abortion.* Nashville,TN: Abingdon Press, 1993.

———. ed., *The Right Choice.* Nashville, TN: Abingdon Press, 1997.

———. ed., *Thinking Theologically About Abortion.* Andersen, IN: Bristol House, LTD, 2000.

"Statement on Abortion from the 39th General Assembly 1972, Minutes, page 17–18, 149," from the Orthodox Presbyterian Church website. Willow Grove, PA, May 15–20, 1972 [cited 6 August 2007]; available from http://opc.org/GA/Abortion_GA39.html; INTERNET.

Tone, Andrea, ed. *Controlling Reproduction: An American History.* Wilmington, DE: SR Books, 1997.

Wald, Kenneth D. *Religion and Politics in the United States.* Washington, D.C.: CQ Press, 1992.

Wesley, John. *Journal of John Wesley,* vol. 1. Chicago: Moody Press, 1951.

———. *Journal of John Wesley, AM.* ed. by Nehemiah Currock, vol. 1. London: The Epworth Press, 1960.

White-Hammond, Gloria Elaine MD, and Ray Hammond, MD. "Consideration of the Abortion Issue," in *AME Working Papers,* III-1—II-24. Nashville, TN: African Methodist Episcopal Church, 1977.

Willimon, William H. "The Ministry of Hospitality," in *The Church and Abortion,* ed. by Paul T. Stallsworth, 17–24. Nashville: Abingdon Press, 1993.

Subject Index